JOHN MAYER
ROOM FOR SQUARES

Piano/Vocal arrangements by John Nicholas

Cover photography by Joshua Kessler
Interior photography by Attila Hardy / Dreams Awake Music

ISBN 1-57560-614-3

Visit our website at www.cherrylane.com

JOHN MAYER

Since the release of his major label debut, *Room for Squares*, in 2001, 25-year-old singer/songwriter John Mayer has become a full-fledged phenomenon, slowly rising from obscurity to stardom, and doing it on his own terms.

His memorable first single, "No Such Thing," begins with the recollection of a life lesson from a high school guidance counselor: "Welcome to the real world/She said to me/Condescendingly." Mayer's ascent proves that the real world can occasionally be bent into unlikely, wondrous shapes. As of this writing, *Squares* has passed the two million plateau and continues selling tens of thousands every week, while Mayer has moved from solo sets in listening rooms to rapid sellouts of 10,000-seat amphitheaters. And this is no flavor-of-the-month, fast-burn success story; his still-growing stardom is based on substance. In an age of ephemera, Mayer is a bona fide career artist, and there's no doubt that this guy is making a connection.

Mayer has built a passionate fan base, from adoring teenagers to discerning boomers who've finally encountered a young artist who lives up to their decades-old memories. The lack, until recently, of media attention and next-big-thing status have actually been a benefit to this aspiring artist, allowing him to fly under the radar and enabling people to discover him in an organic way, thus forming a bond between performer and fan that is extremely rare in this fickle era. Reviewing Mayer's L.A. House of Blues set in April 2002, Bud Scoppa of *HITS Daily Double* noted, "Perhaps the most remarkable single aspect of the show was the way the crowd sang along with every word, in tune and in unison, so locked in that it sounded rehearsed. I've never seen an audience more hooked up with an artist."

Mayer, who grew up in Fairfield, CT, by way of Bridgeport, is the second of three children born to an English teacher mother and high school principal father. His first musical epiphany came at age 13, when he discovered Stevie Ray Vaughan, then badgered his dad into getting him an electric guitar. The kid turned out to be a quick study: two years later he was doing solo turns in local clubs. After high school, Mayer spent a few months at Boston's Berklee School of Music before dropping out and moving to Atlanta, where he quickly clicked on the area's club circuit. During this time, he began amalgamating the key elements of his influences—notably, Vaughan, Hendrix, Clapton, Elton John, Ben Folds, and Dave Matthews—into a wide-open approach that somehow meshed fluent guitar playing, fat grooves, conversational narratives, heady improvisation, and emphatic hooks into a remarkably expressive whole.

"Connecticut's where I built the parts, Boston's where I assembled them, and Atlanta is where I sold them to people," he quipped about his own *Field of Dreams* scenario.

In 1999 Mayer cut *Inside Wants Out* (reissued by Columbia in 2002) to sell at his shows. What's startling about these early solo performances is how utterly complete they are, a vivid testament to his elevated songcraft and to the rich, expressive guitar style he'd developed by that time. Indeed, Mayer's guitar lines on the early versions of "No Such Thing," "My Stupid Mouth," and "Neon" provided detailed blueprints for the full-band arrangements on *Room for Squares*.

The buzz spread across the South, and caught the ear of the record biz, when Mayer played a masterful set at Austin's South by Southwest (SxSW) Music Conference in March 2000. Soon afterward, he signed with Aware Records and began traversing the U.S. and winning over fans one by one, night by night, while recording his first official album with producer John Alagia (Dave Matthews, Ben Folds) between legs on what would turn out to be two full years of touring.

He decided to call the album *Room for Squares*, a characteristically wry take on jazz sax player Hank Mobley's 1963 LP *No Room for Squares*. "It made sense to me because I feel unsteady in coolness," he explained.

The album initially came out as an indie release on Aware in the spring of 2001 and was reissued by Columbia four months later, with the addition of the stunning track "3X5," new packaging and a limited edition bonus EP featuring covers of songs by Jimi Hendrix and Stevie Ray Vaughan. By year's end, the media began to pick up the scent. In a benchmark review that December in *Rolling Stone*, critic Anthony DeCurtis proclaimed the album "instantly likable and accessible. But it's no less smart and affecting for that. These thirteen songs are a travelogue of discovery, of love, identity, and purpose."

Then, in 2002, all hell broke loose, and John Mayer broke through.

"Every day someone says to me, 'I just want you to know this never happens,'" Mayer said last April. "And I go, 'Well, what do you mean? It's happening to me.'"

CONTENTS

No Such Thing

Words by John Mayer

Music by
John Mayer and Clay Cook

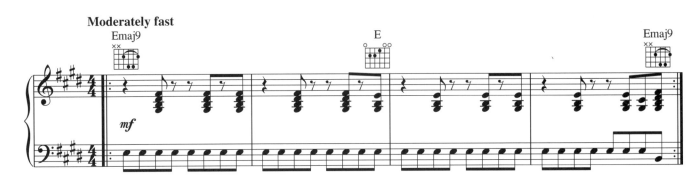

"Wel - come to the real __ world," she said to me con - de - scend -

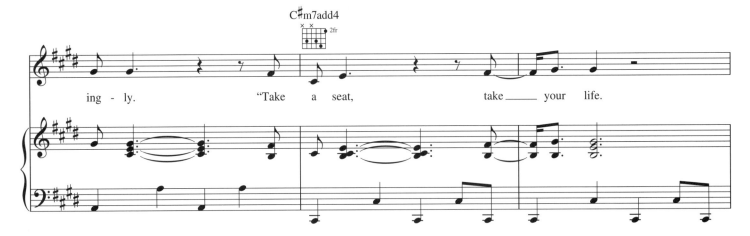

ing - ly. "Take a seat, take __ your life.

Plot it out __ in black __ and white." __ Well, I

nev - er lived the dreams of the prom____ kings____ and the dra - ma queens.__ I'd like to think the

best of me____ is still hid - ing up my__ sleeve.____ They

love to tell you "Stay in - side the lines."____

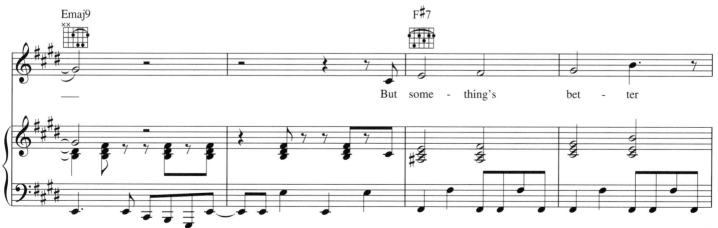

But some - thing's bet - ter

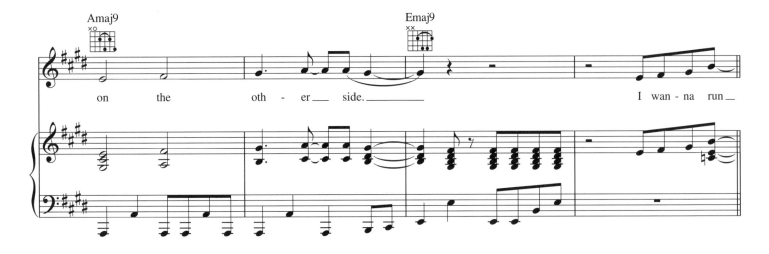

on the oth-er____ side._____ I wan-na run____

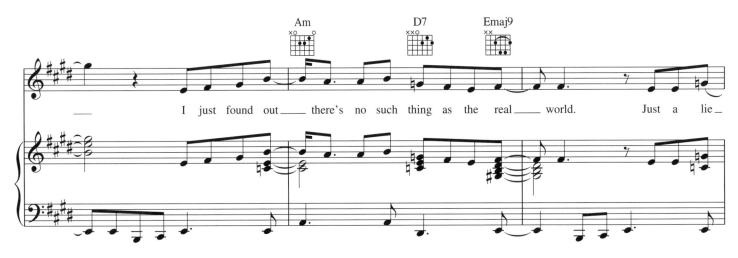

____ through the halls____ of my high____ school. I wan-na scream____ at the top of my lungs.____

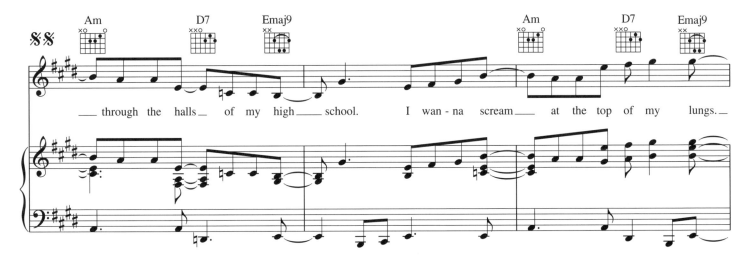

____ I just found out____ there's no such thing as the real____ world. Just a lie____

To Codas I and II

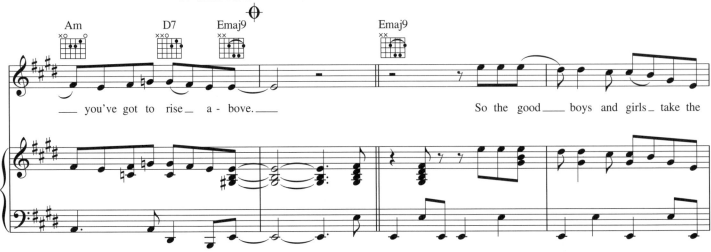

____ you've got to rise____ a - bove.____ So the good____ boys and girls____ take the

so-called right track, fad-ed white hats, grab-bing cred-its and may-be trans-fers. They

read all the books__ but they can't__ find the an-swers.__ And all of our par-

ents,__ they're get-ting old-er. I won-der if they've wished for an-y-thing

bet-ter__ while in their mem-'ries,__ ti-ny trag-e-dies.__

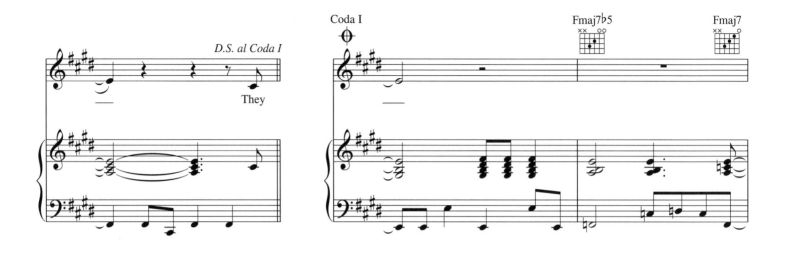

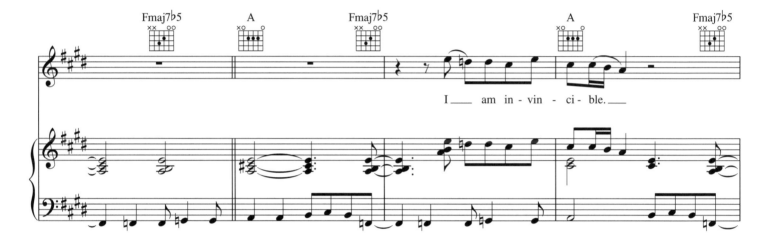

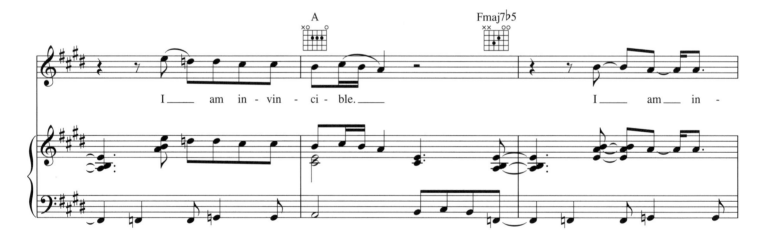

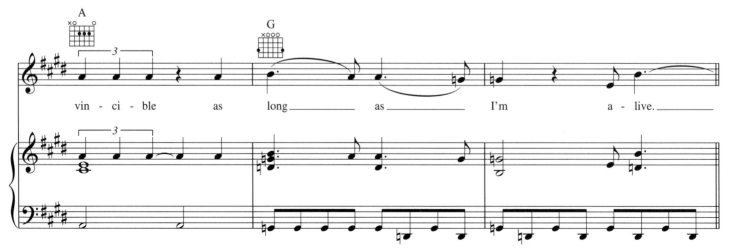

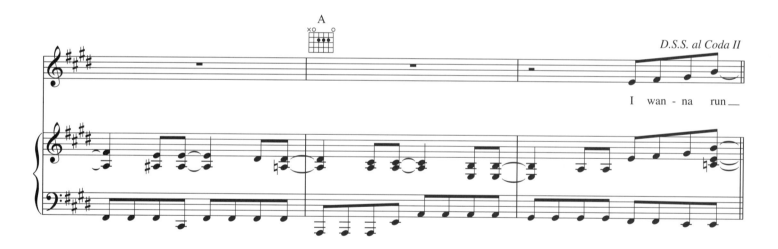

I wan - na run___

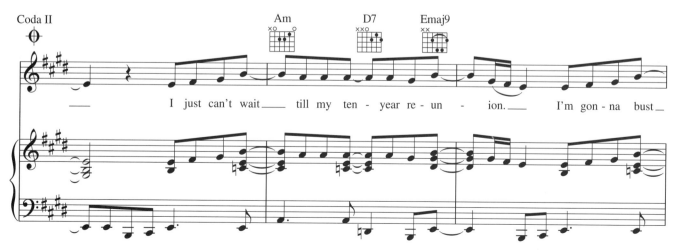

I just can't wait___ till my ten - year re - un - ion.___ I'm gon - na bust___

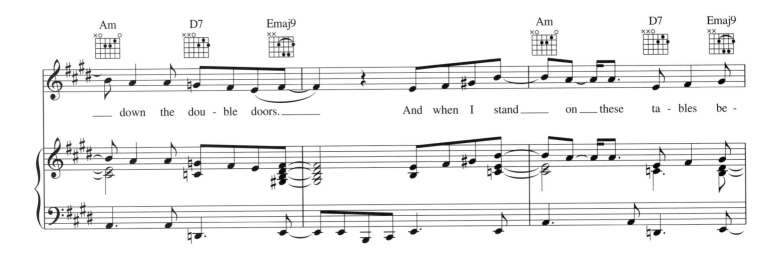

___ down the dou - ble doors.___ And when I stand__ on __ these ta - bles be -

fore you, you will know__ what all this time was____ for.

with pedal

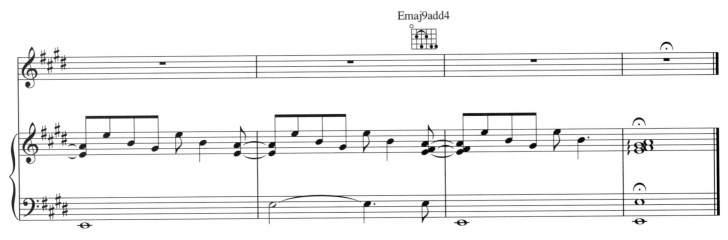

Why Georgia

Words and Music by
John Mayer

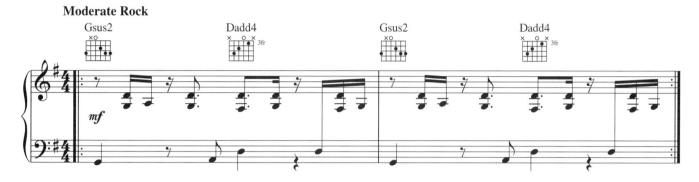

I ___ am driv-ing ___ up Eight-y-five in ___ the
Four ___ more ex-its ___ to my ___ a-part-ment, ___ but

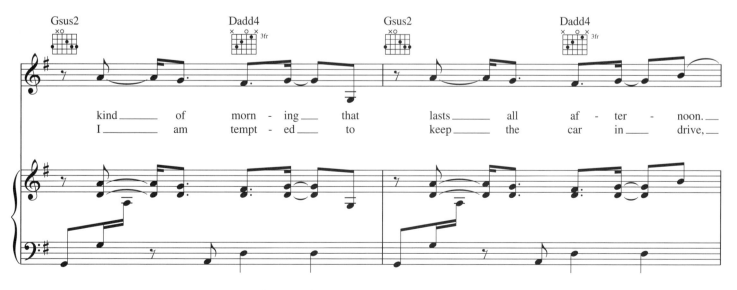

kind ___ of morn-ing ___ that lasts ___ all af-ter-noon. ___
I ___ am tempt-ed ___ to keep ___ the car in ___ drive, ___

I'm just stuck in - side the gloom.
and leave it all be - hind.

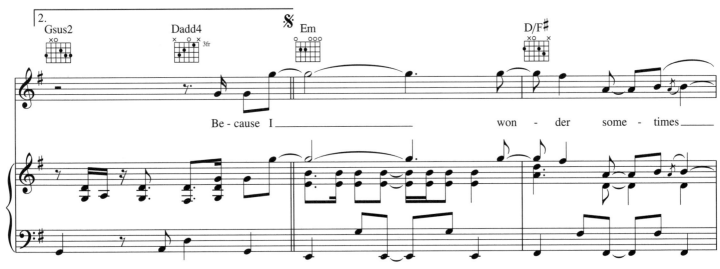

Be - cause I won - der some - times

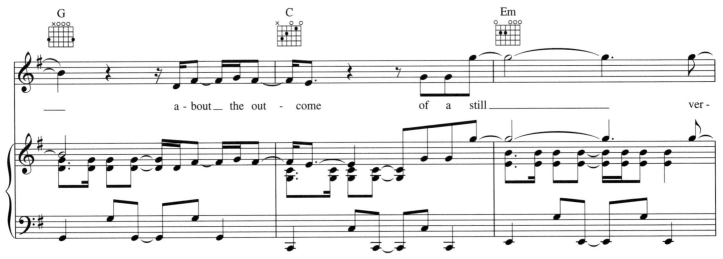

a - bout the out - come of a still ver -

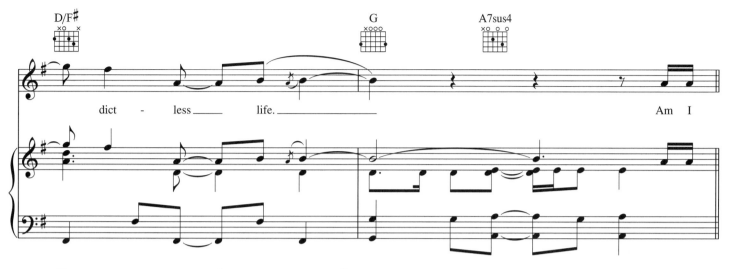

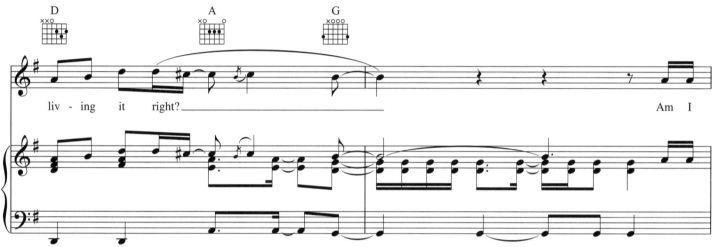

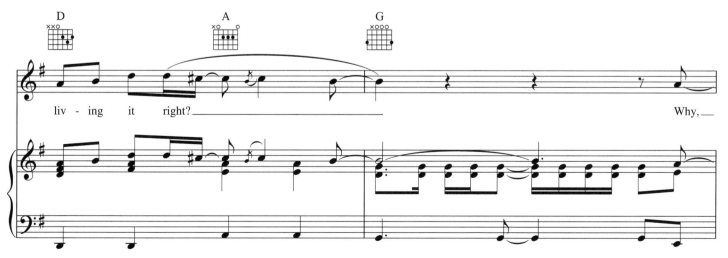

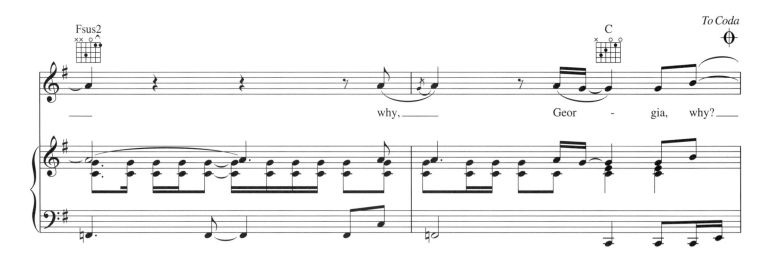

why, _____ Geor - gia, why? _____

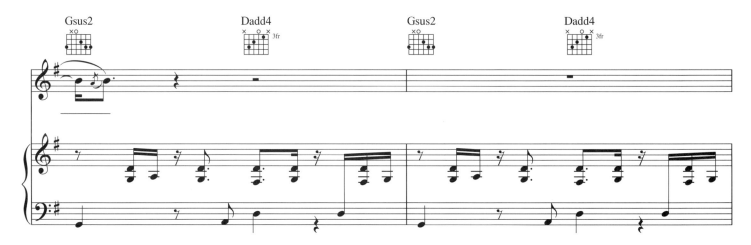

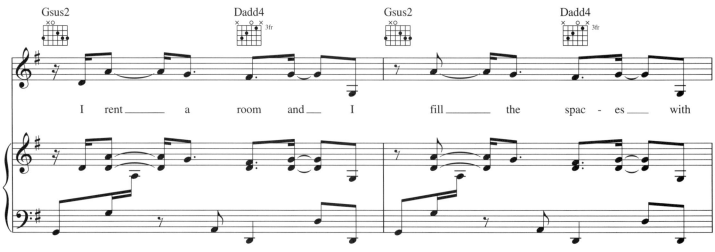

I rent _____ a room and _____ I fill _____ the spac - es _____ with

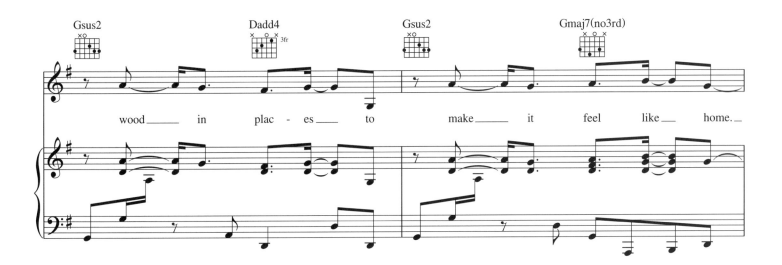

wood ___ in plac - es ___ to make ___ it feel like ___ home. ___

___ But all ___ I feel's ___ a - lone. ___

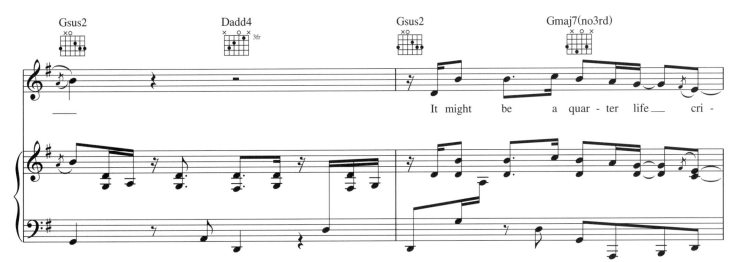

___ It might be a quar - ter life ___ cri -

sis, ___ or just the stir - ring in ___ my ___

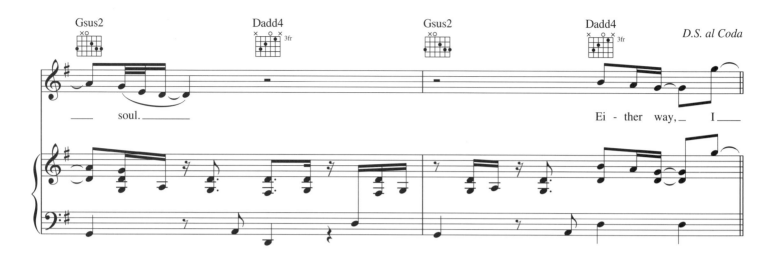

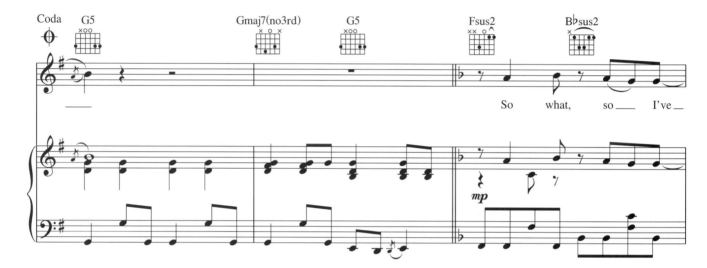

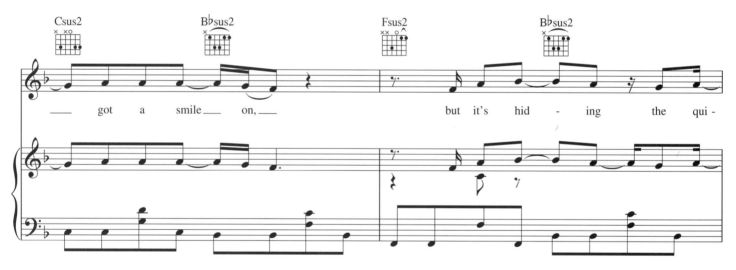

16

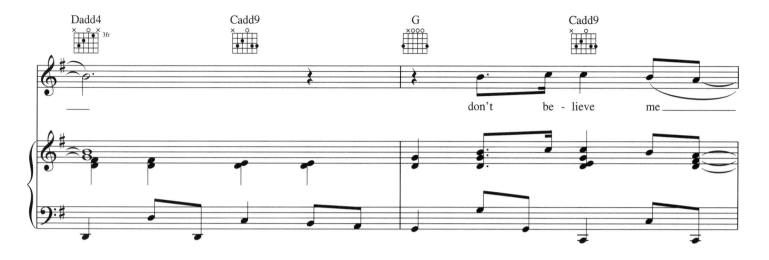

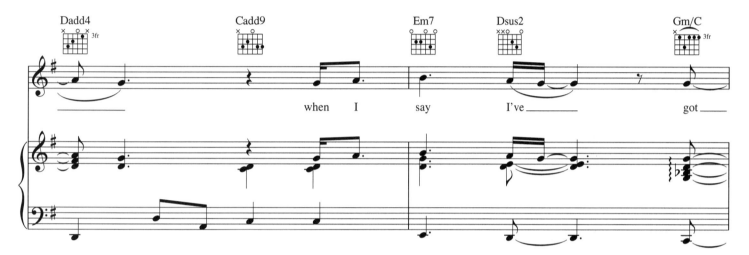

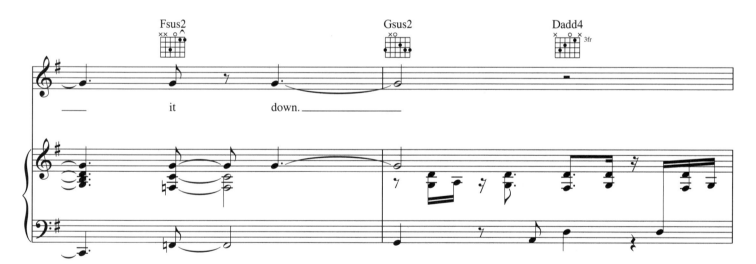

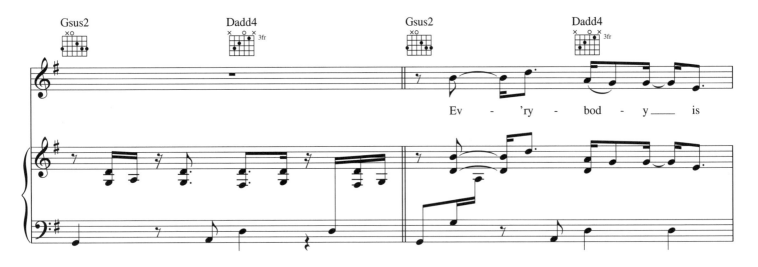

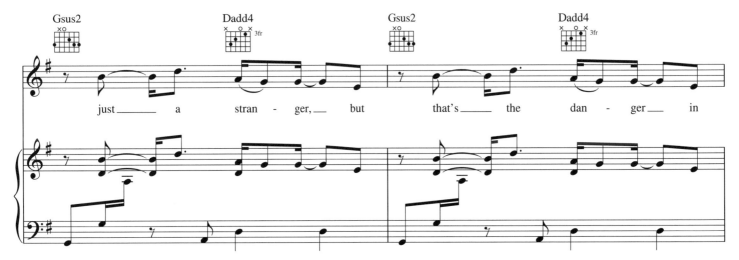

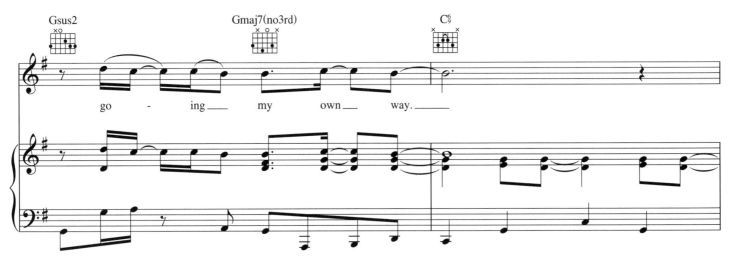

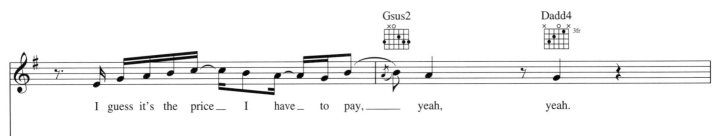

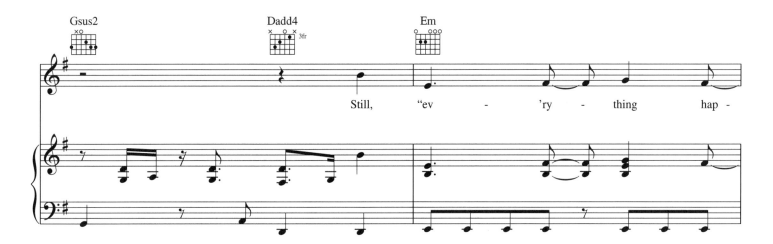

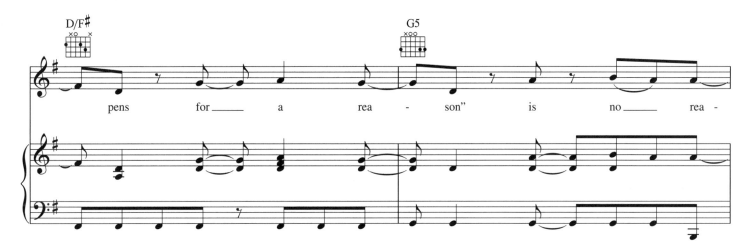

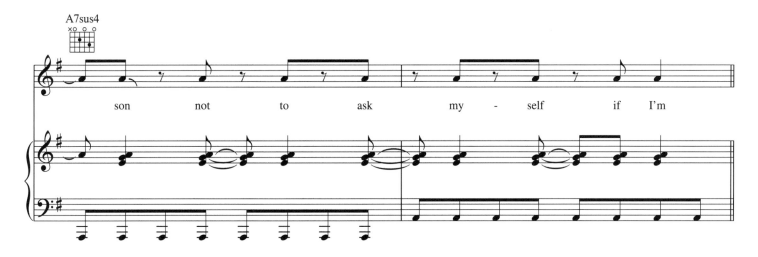

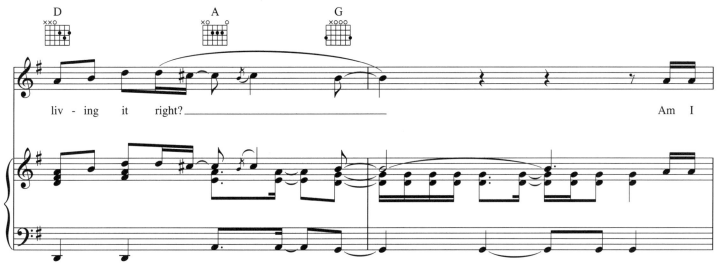

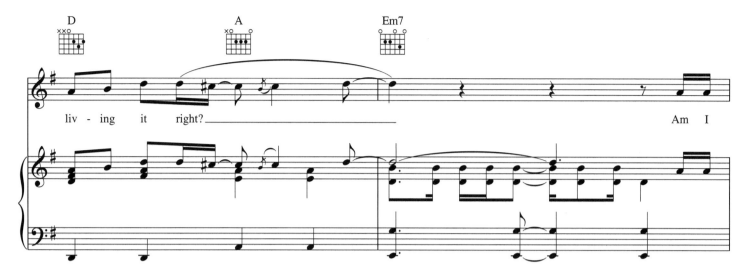

liv - ing it right?_____ Am I

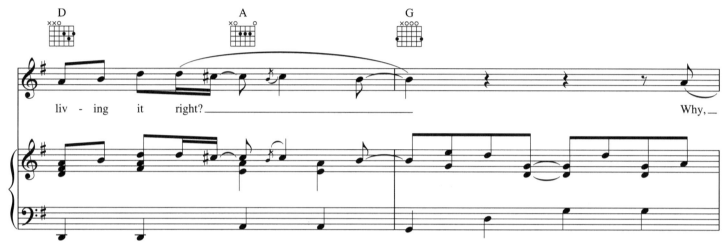

liv - ing it right?_____ Why,_

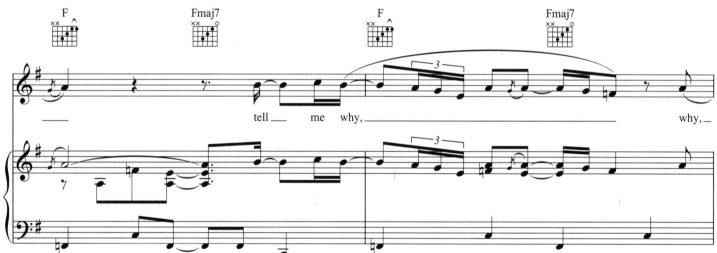

____ tell ___ me why,_____ why,_

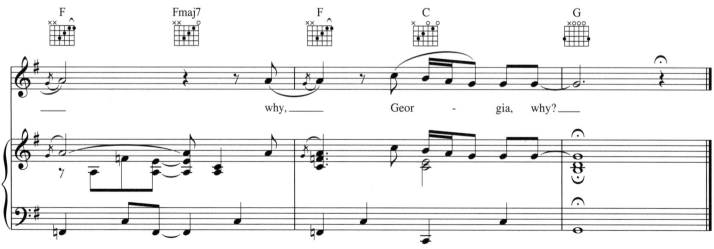

____ why,_____ Geor - gia, why?___

My Stupid Mouth

Words and Music by
John Mayer

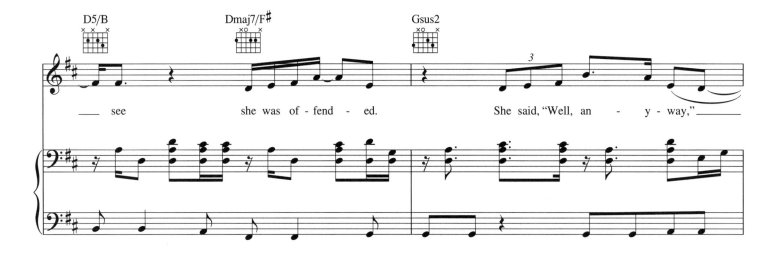

see she was of-fend-ed. She said, "Well, an - y - way,"

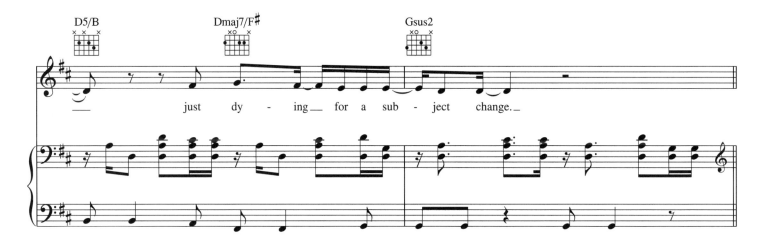

just dy - ing for a sub - ject change.

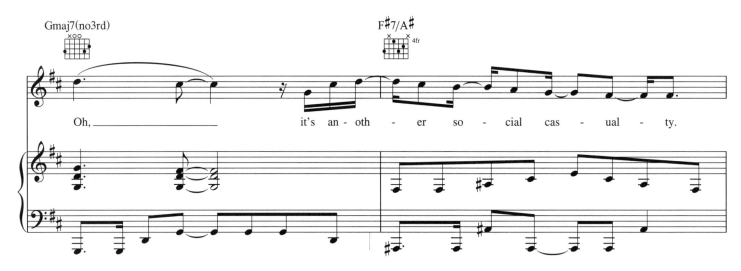

Oh, it's an-oth - er so - cial cas - ual - ty.

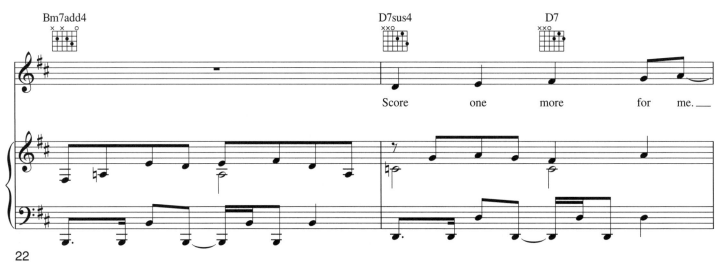

Score one more for me.

We bit our lips. She looked out the win - dow, __

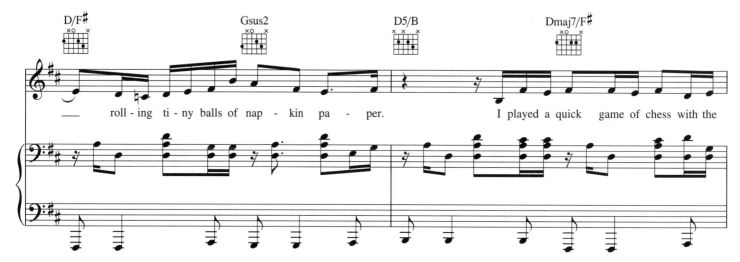

__ roll - ing ti - ny balls of nap - kin pa - per. I played a quick game of chess with the

salt and pep - per shak - er. __ And I could see clear - ly __

an in - del - i - ble line was __ drawn be - tween what __ was good, __ what just __

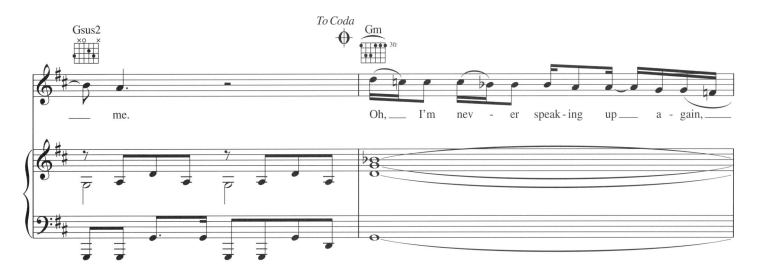

me. Oh, I'm nev - er speak-ing up a - gain,

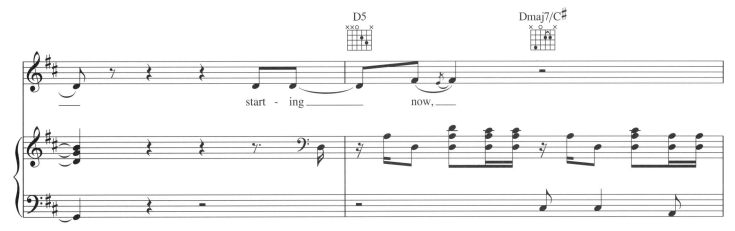

start - ing now,

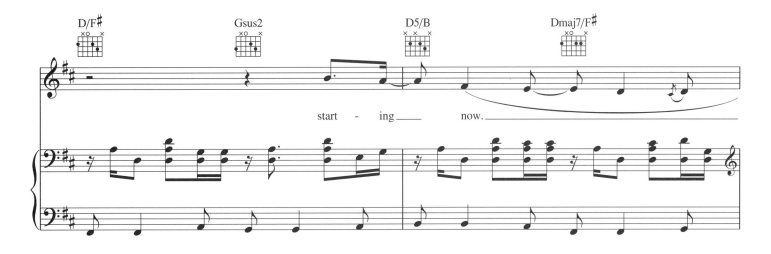

start - ing now.

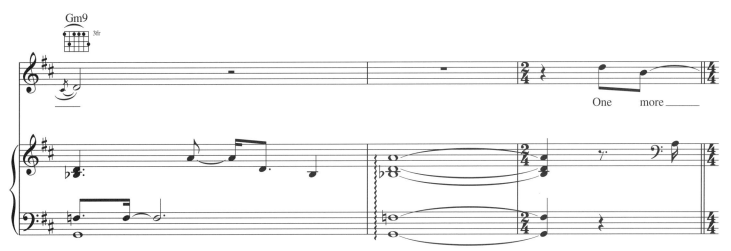

One more

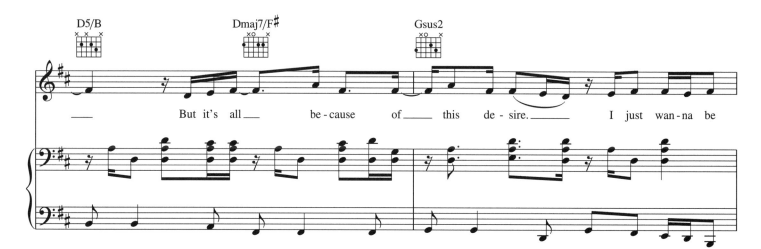

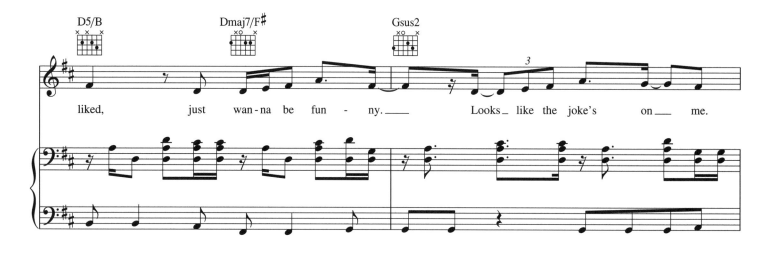

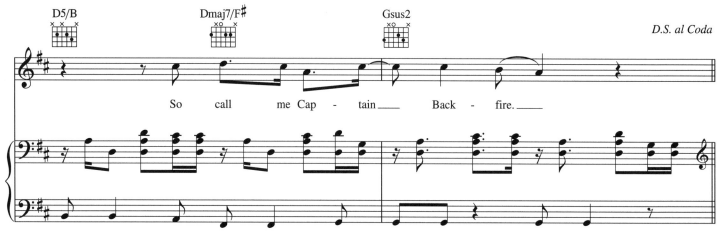

Your Body Is a Wonderland

Words and Music by
John Mayer

We got___ the af-ter-noon.___ You got___ this room___
One mile___ to ev-'ry inch of your skin,___ like por -

___ for two.___ One thing___ I've left to do: dis -
ce - lain.___ One pair___ of can - dy lips___ and your

cov - er me ___ dis - cov - er - ing you. ___

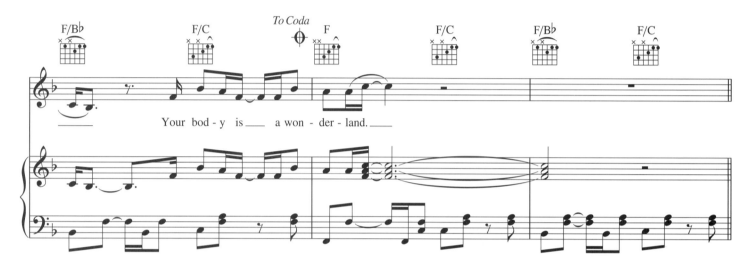

You tell__ me where__ to go,__ and though I___ might leave__ to find__ it, I'll

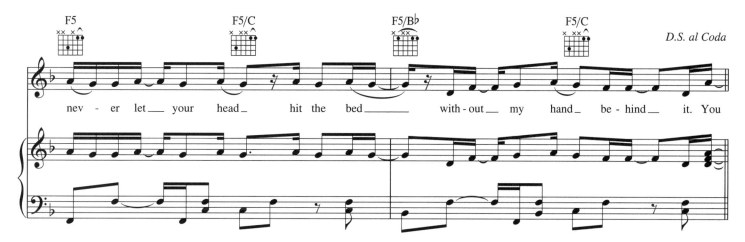

D.S. al Coda

nev - er let__ your head__ hit the bed_____ with-out__ my hand__ be-hind__ it. You

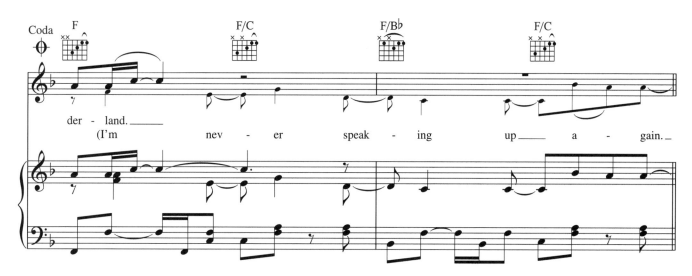

Coda

der - land._____
(I'm nev - er speak - ing up____ a - gain.__

Dm9

____ I'll__ use__ my__ hands.)_____

Damn, ba - by._____

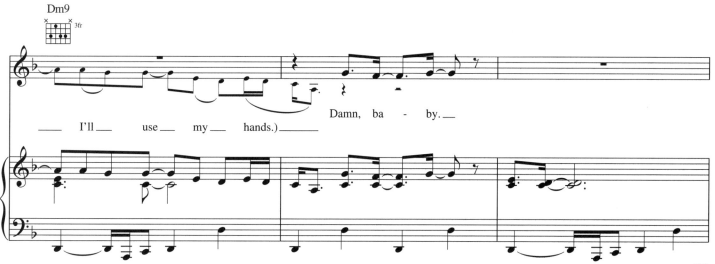

You frus - trate___ me.___   I know you're mine, all_____ mine, all___

mine,_____   but you look___ so good,_ it hurts___ some - times.

Dm9

1.

2.

F5/D

Your bod-y is ____ a won - der - land. _____ Your bod-y is ____ a won -

der. I'll ____ use ____ my ____ hands. _____ Your bod - y is ____ a won -

der - land. ____ Your bod - y is ____ a won - der - land. _____

Repeat and fade

Da da da, da da da da da, da da da, da da da __ da.

Neon

Words by John Mayer

Music by John Mayer
and Clay Cook

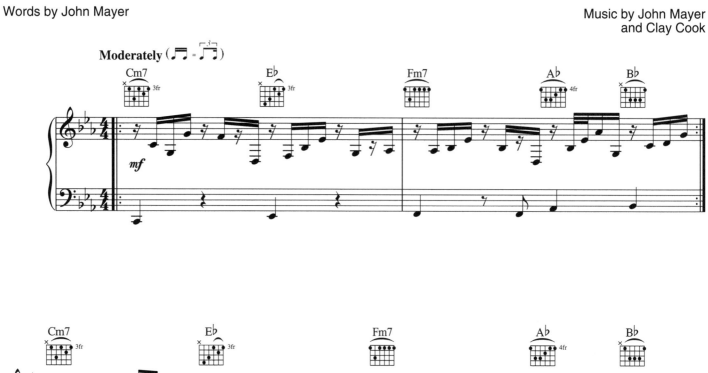

When sky blue_____ gets dark_____ e - nough_

to see the col - ors of the cit - y lights,_____

a trail of ru - by red and dia - mond white __

hits her like a sun - rise. _____ She comes __

__ and goes __ and comes __ and goes __ like no __

__ one can. _____

37

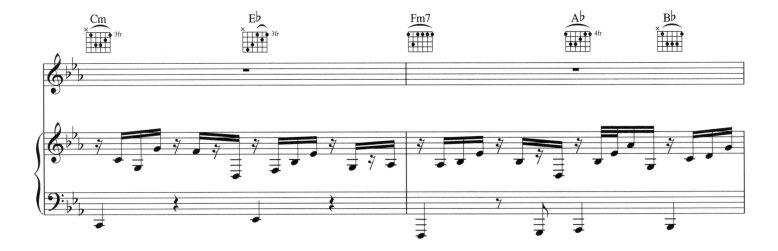

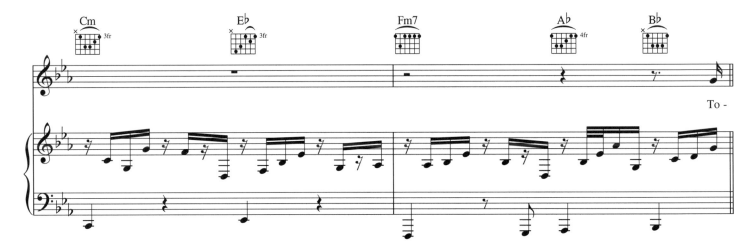

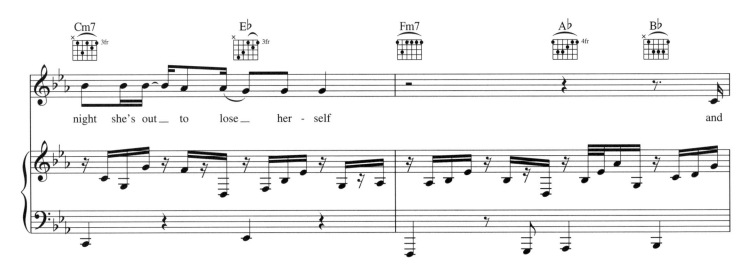

night she's out to lose her-self and

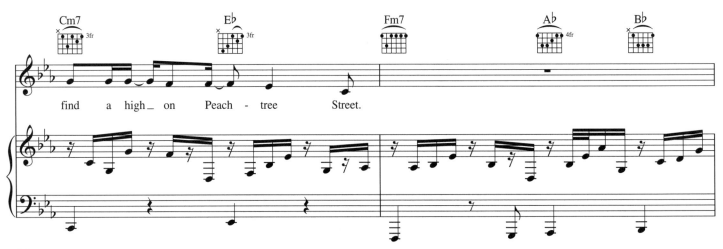

find a high on Peach-tree Street.

From mixed drinks to tech-no beats— it's al - ways—

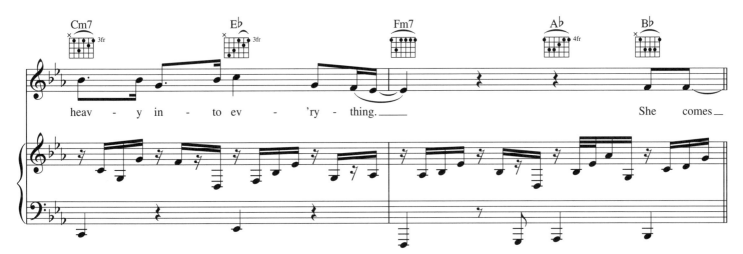

heav - y in - to ev - 'ry - thing.— She comes—

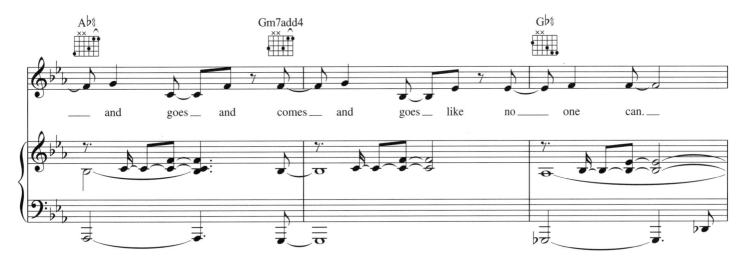

— and goes— and comes— and goes— like no— one can.—

She comes— and goes— and no—

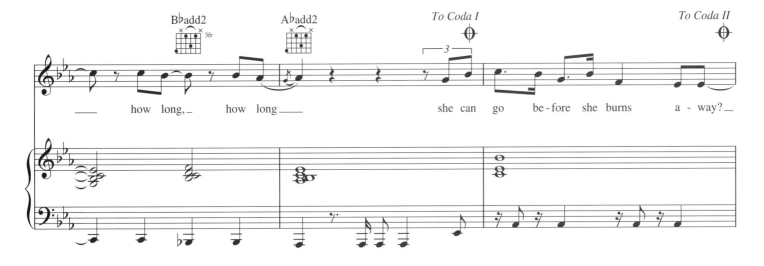

how long,___ how long___ she can go be-fore she burns a-way?___

I can't be ___ her an-gel now.___ You know it's___

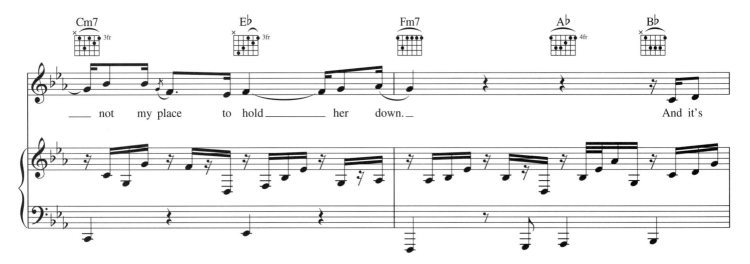

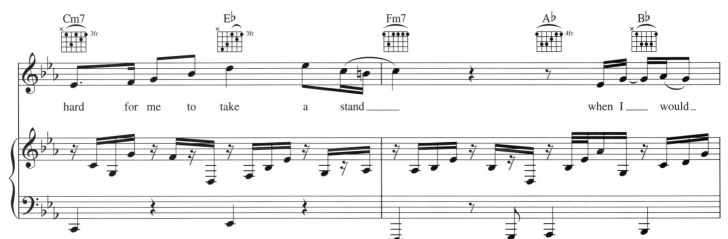

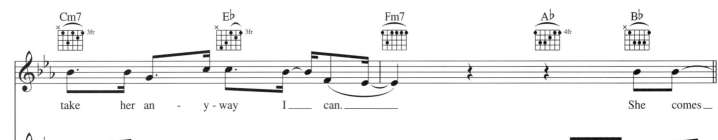

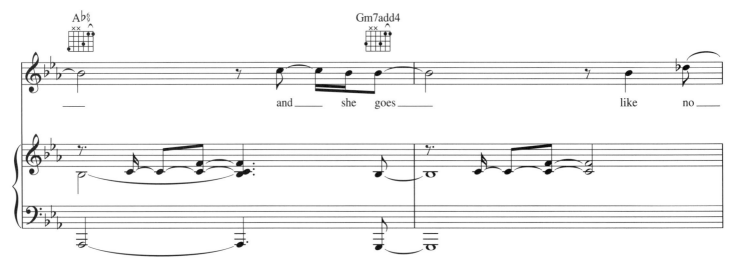

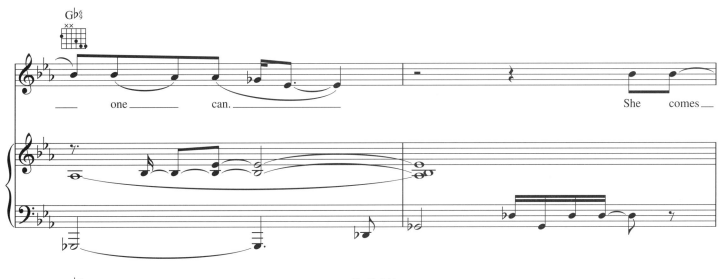

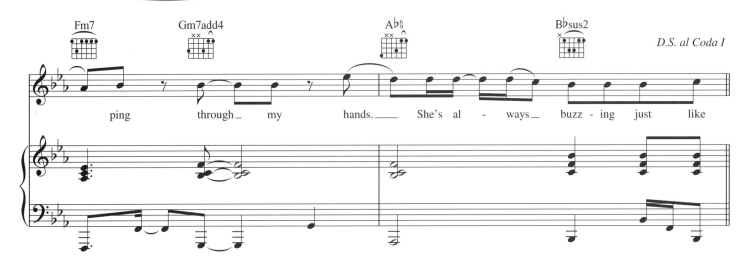

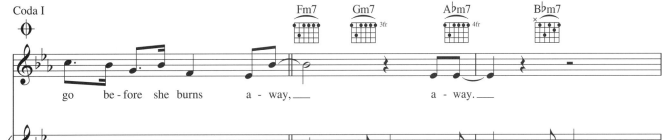

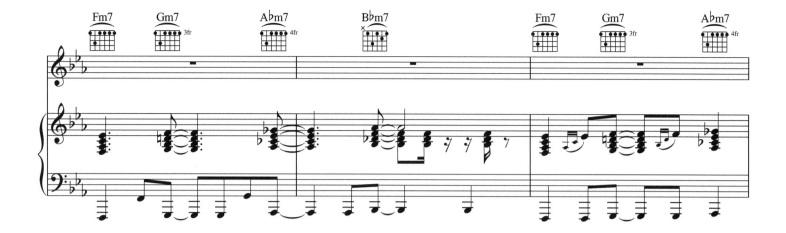

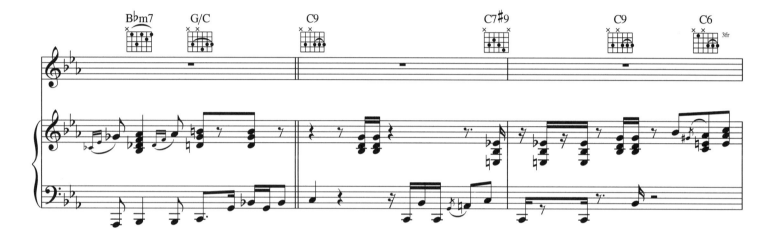

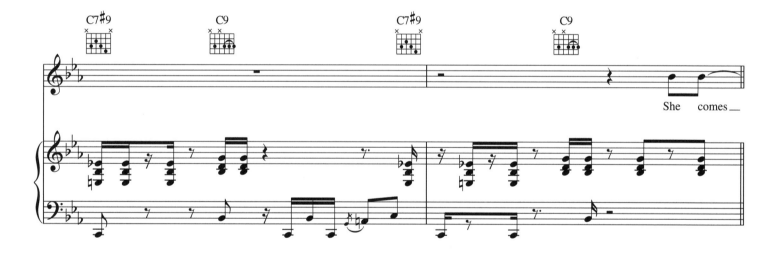

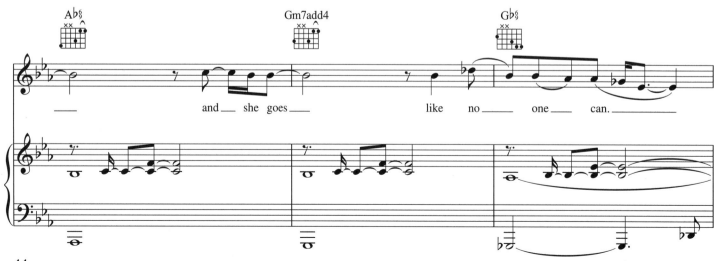

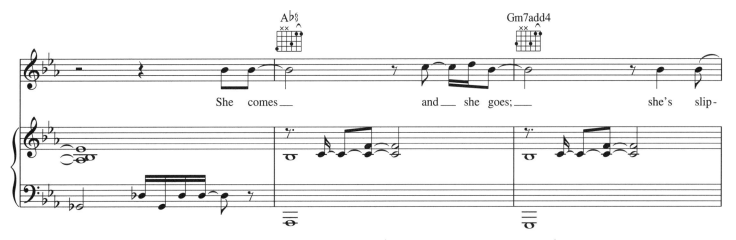

She comes ___ and ___ she goes; ___ she's slip-

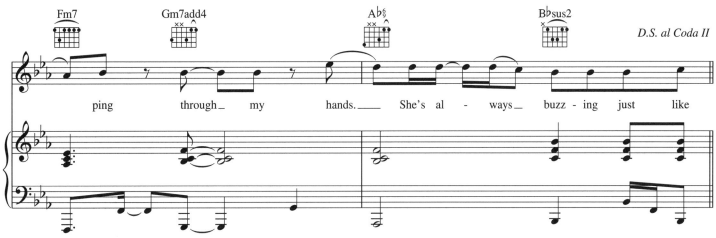

D.S. al Coda II

ping through ___ my hands. ___ She's al - ways ___ buzz - ing just like

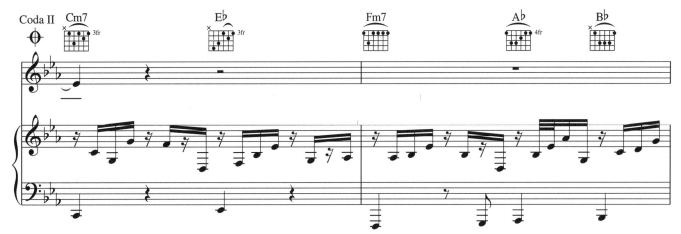

Coda II

Repeat and fade

City Love

Words and Music by
John Mayer

Moderately slow

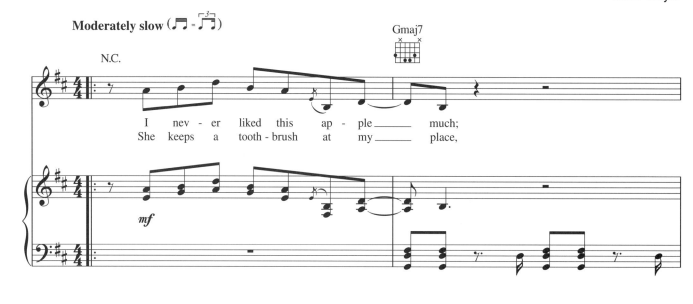

it al-ways seemed too big to _____ touch. _____
as if I had the ex-tra _____ space. _____

I can't re-mem-ber how I _____ found _____
She steals my clothes to wear to _____ work. _____

I nev-er liked this ap-ple _____ much;
She keeps a tooth-brush at my _____ place,

day   she called up and ___ came ___ to me   cov - ered in   rain ___

___ and din - ner - time shad - ow - ing.   And as her clothes ___

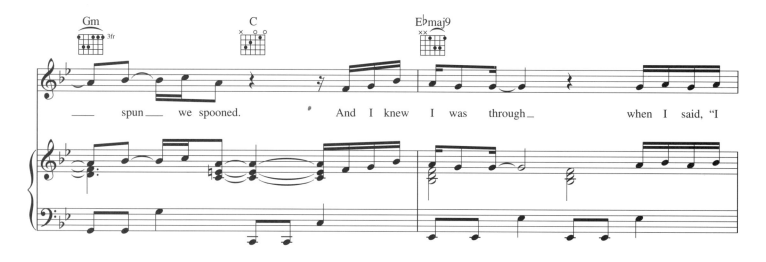

___ spun ___ we spooned.   And I knew I was through ___ when I said, "I

love you." ___

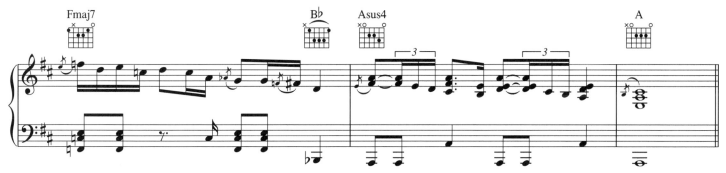

Fri - day eve - ning, we've been drink - ing. Two A. M., I swear I might pro - pose.

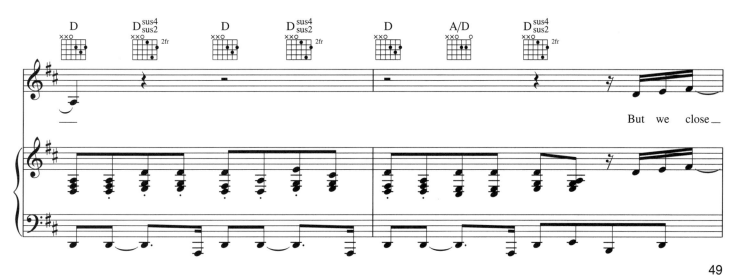

But we close

the tab, split a cab and call each oth-er up when we get home,_____

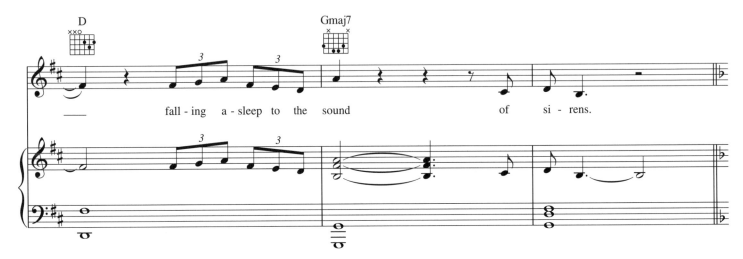

fall-ing a-sleep to the sound of si - rens.

I've got a____ cit - y love;

I found it in____ Lyd - i - a.

83

Words and Music by
John Mayer

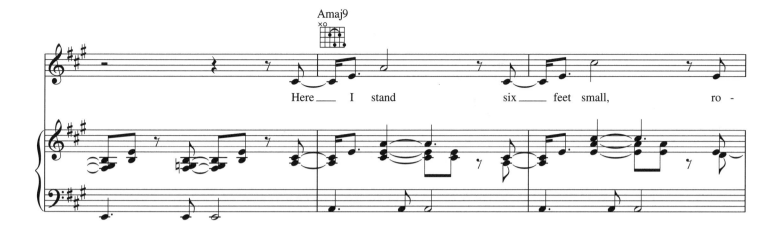

Here __ I stand six __ feet small, ro -

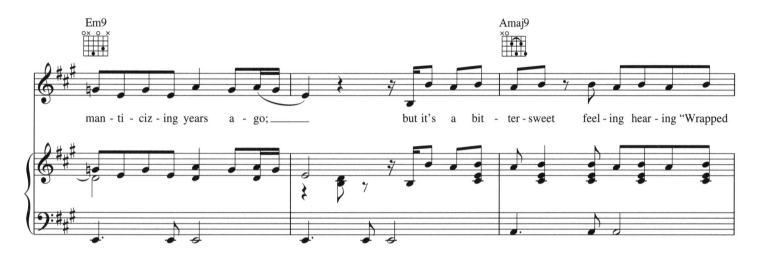

man - ti - ciz - ing years a - go; __ but it's a bit - ter - sweet feel - ing hear - ing "Wrapped

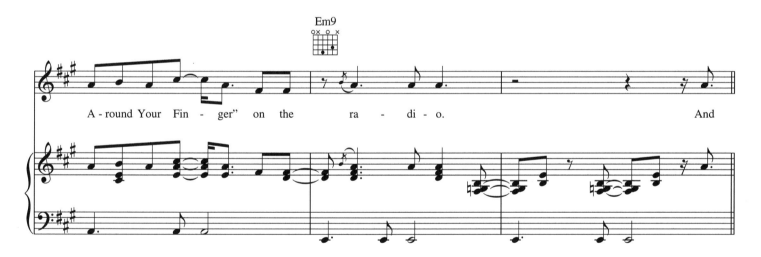

A - round Your Fin - ger" on the ra - di - o. And

these days __ I wish I was six a - gain.

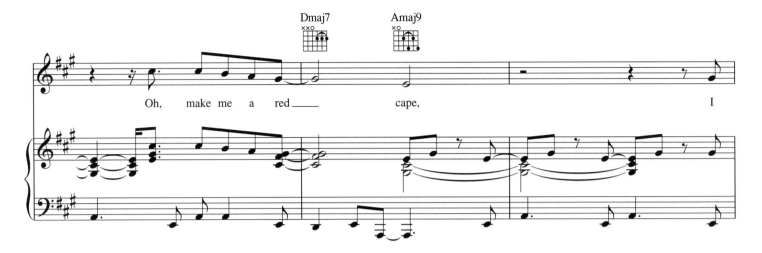

Oh, make me a red____ cape, I

wan-na be Su-per-man. Oh, if on-ly my life_____ was more_ like nine-

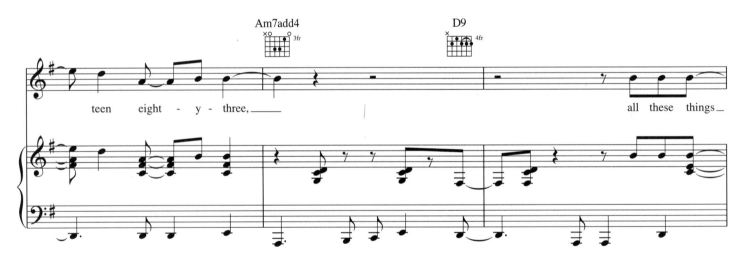

teen eight-y-three,_____ all these things_

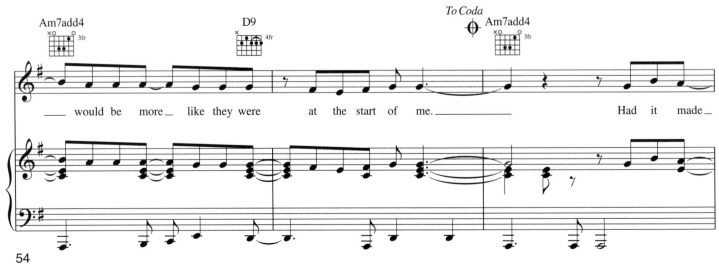

____ would be more_ like they were at the start of me._____ Had it made_

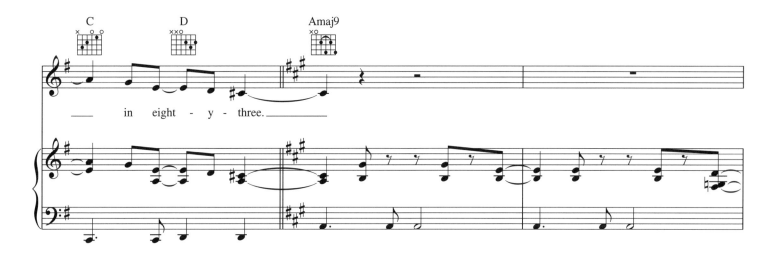

_____ in eight - y - three. _____

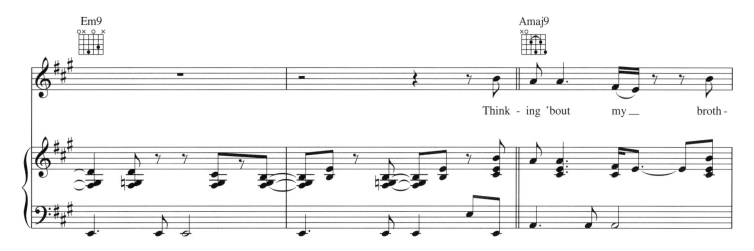

Think - ing 'bout my _____ broth -

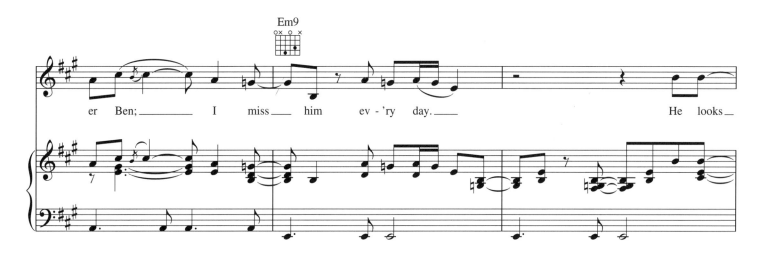

er Ben; _____ I miss _____ him ev - 'ry day. _____ He looks _____

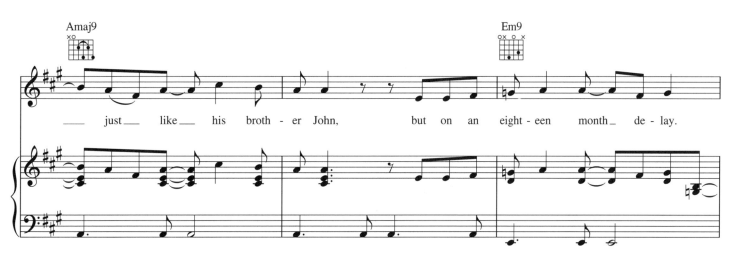

_____ just _____ like _____ his broth - er John, but on an eigh - teen month _ de - lay.

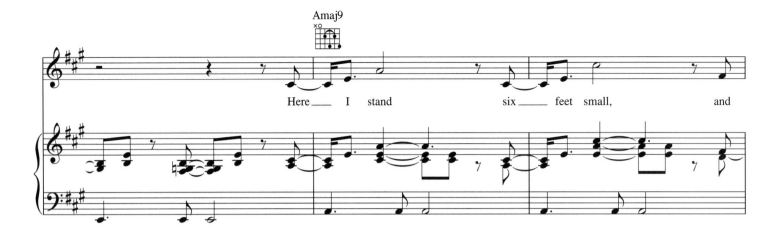

Here___ I stand six___ feet small, and

smil-ing 'cause I'm scared as hell.___ Kind of like my life is like a se-

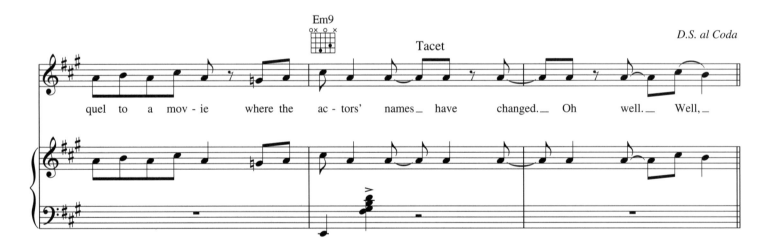

quel to a mov-ie where the ac-tors' names___ have changed.___ Oh well.___ Well,___

D.S. al Coda

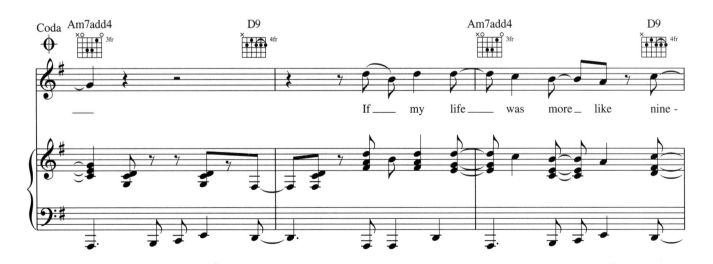

___ If___ my life___ was more___ like nine-

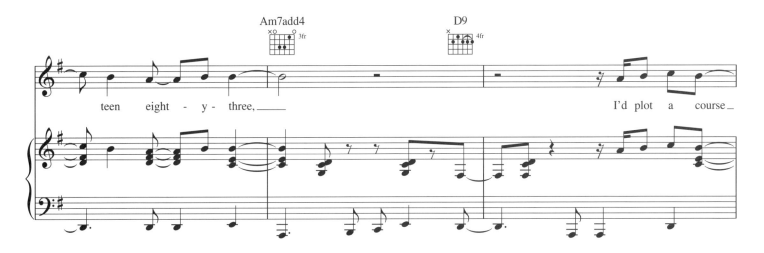

teen eight - y - three,_____ I'd plot a course_____

_____ to the source_____ of the pur - est lit - tle_____ part of me._____

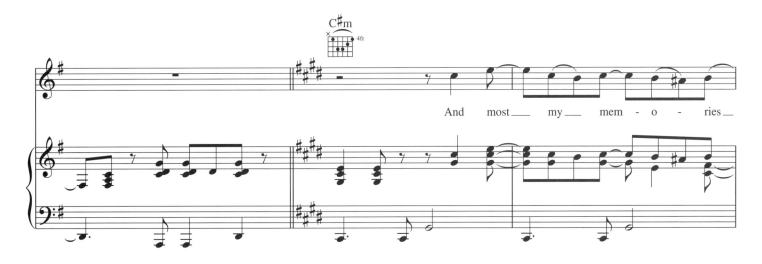

And most_____ my_____ mem - o - ries_____

have es - caped_____ me or con - fused_____

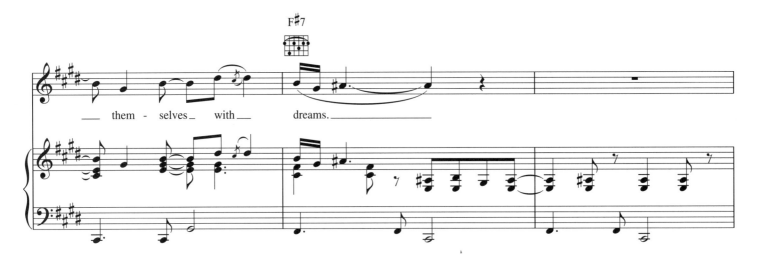

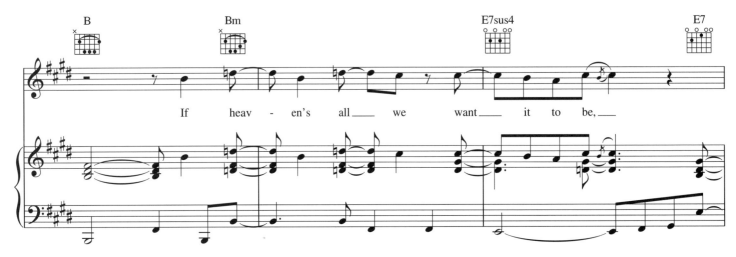

them - selves with dreams.

If heav - en's all we want it to be,

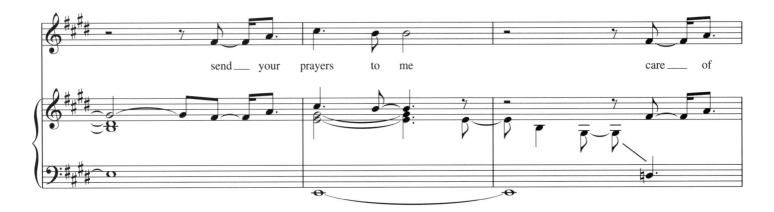

send your prayers to me care of

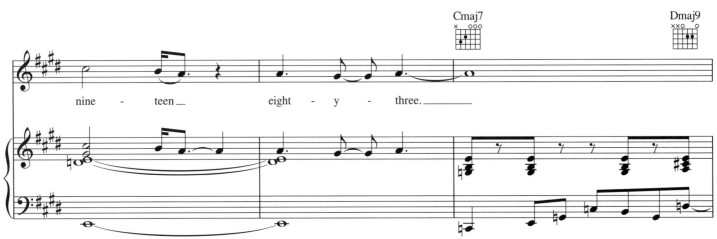

nine - teen eight - y - three.

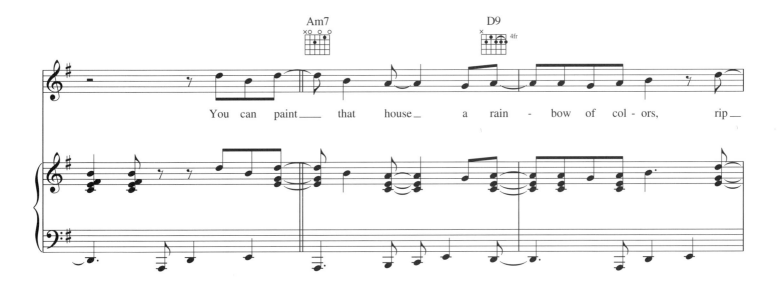

You can paint___ that house___ a rain - bow of col - ors,___ rip___

___ out___ the floor - boards, re - place the shut - ters, but_____ that's___ my plas -

59

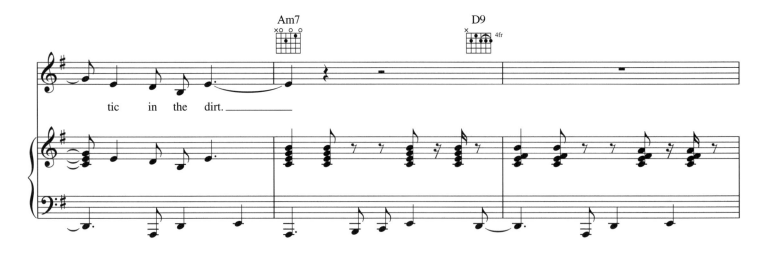

tic in the dirt. _____

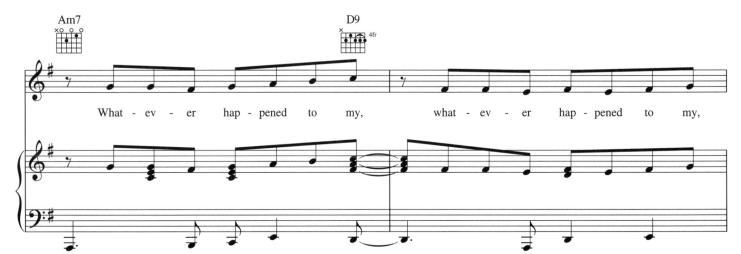

What - ev - er hap - pened to my, what - ev - er hap - pened to my,

what - ev - er hap - pened to my lunch - box? _____

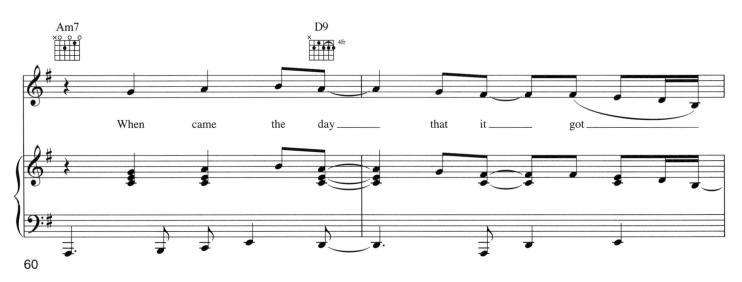

When came the day _____ that it _____ got _____

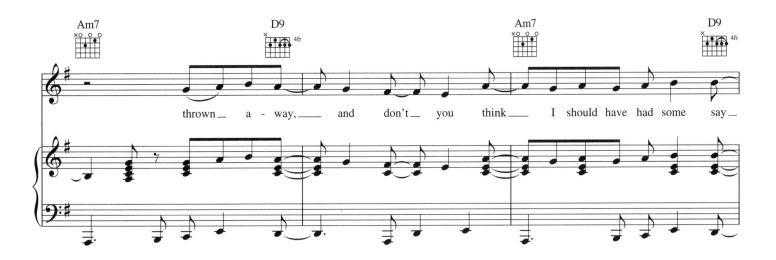

thrown__ a - way,__ and don't__ you think__ I should have had some say__

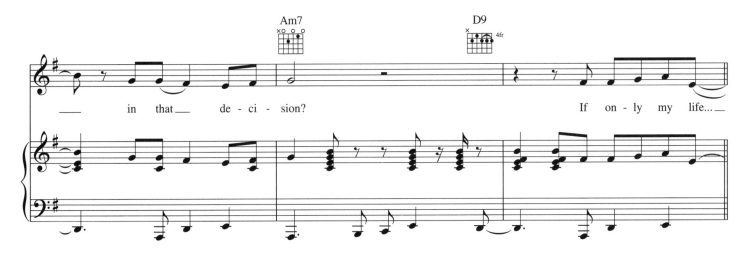

__ in that__ de - ci - sion? If on - ly my life...__

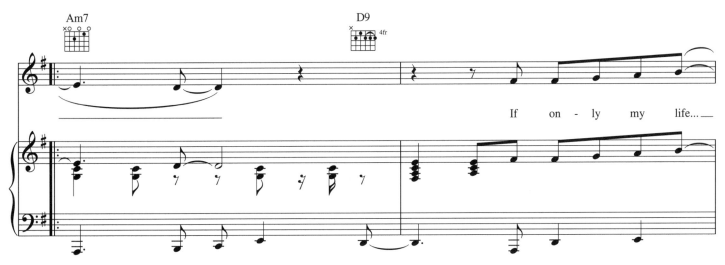

If on - ly my life...__

Repeat and fade

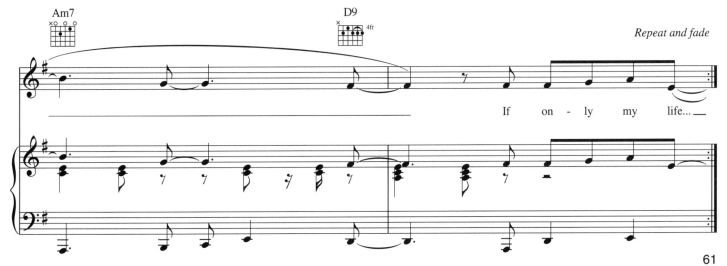

If on - ly my life...__

3X5

Words and Music by
John Mayer

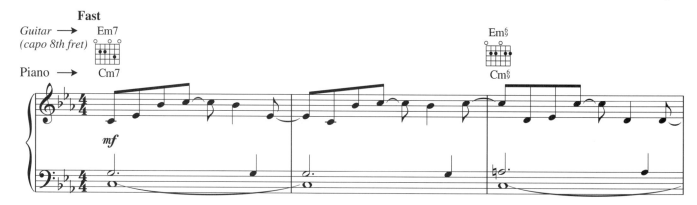

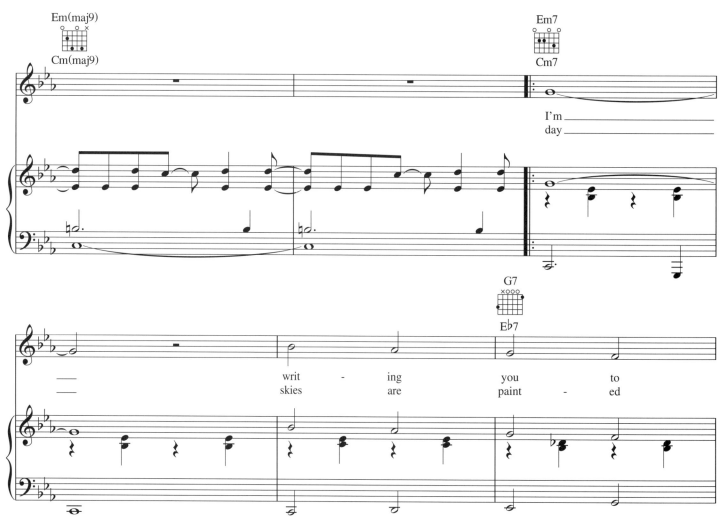

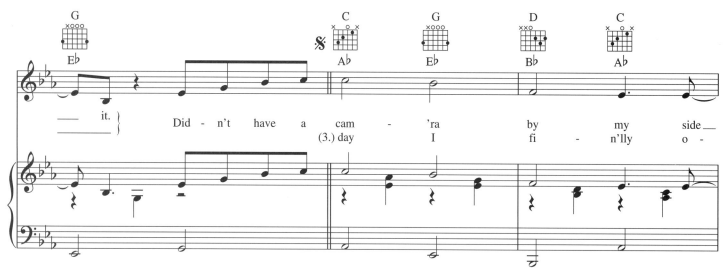

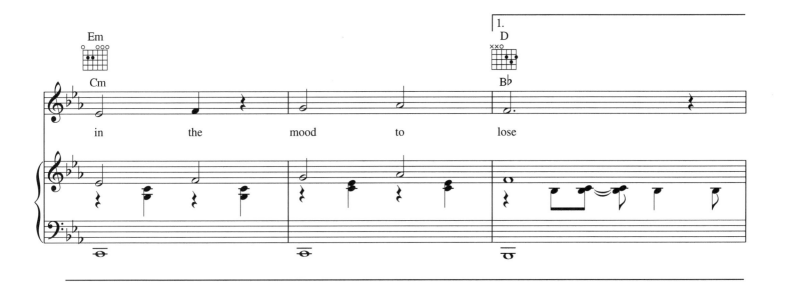

in   the   mood   to   lose

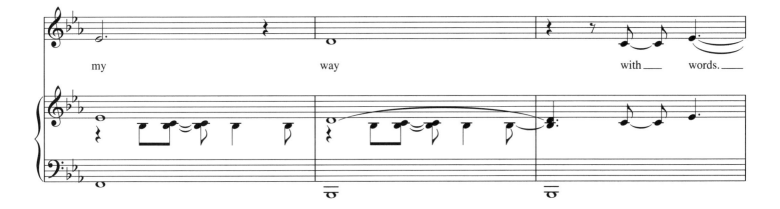

my   way   with ___ words. ___

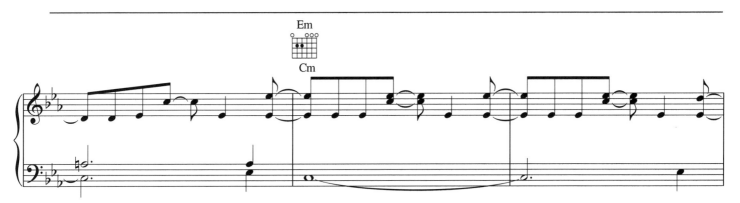

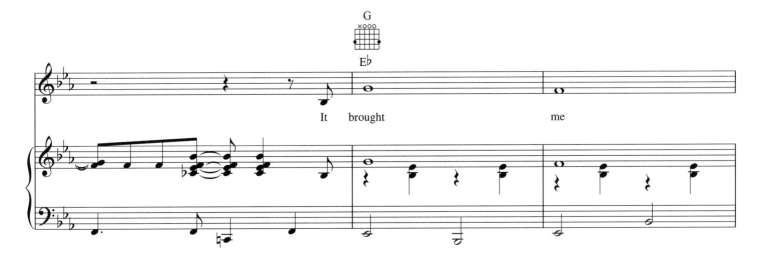

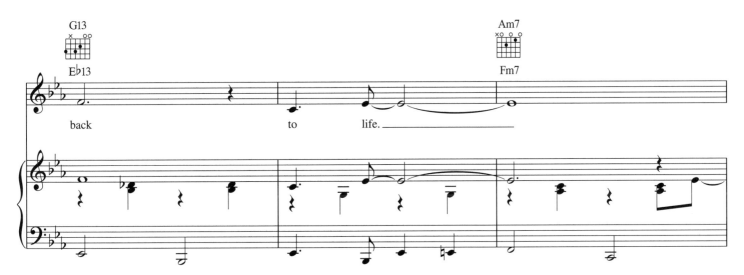

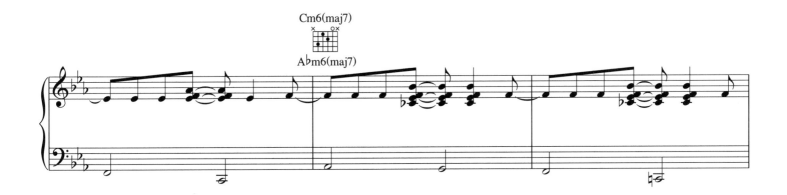

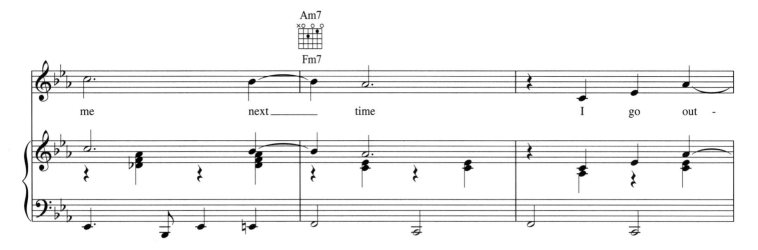

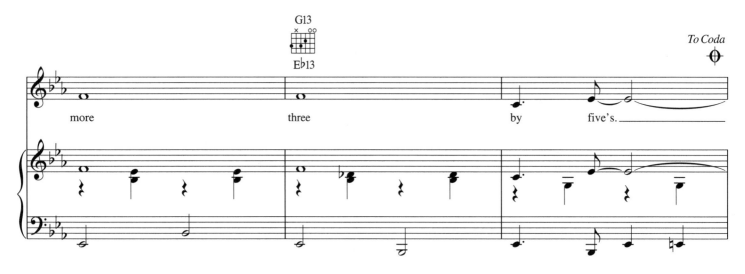

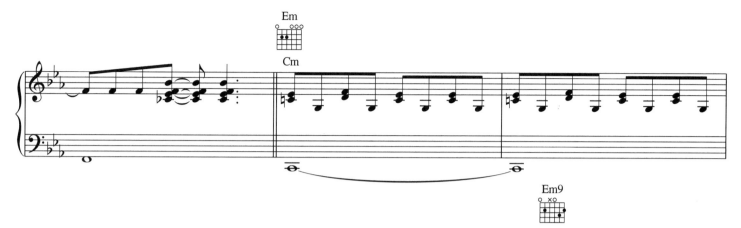

guess you had to

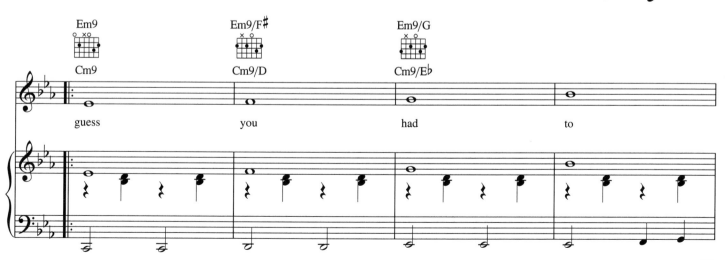

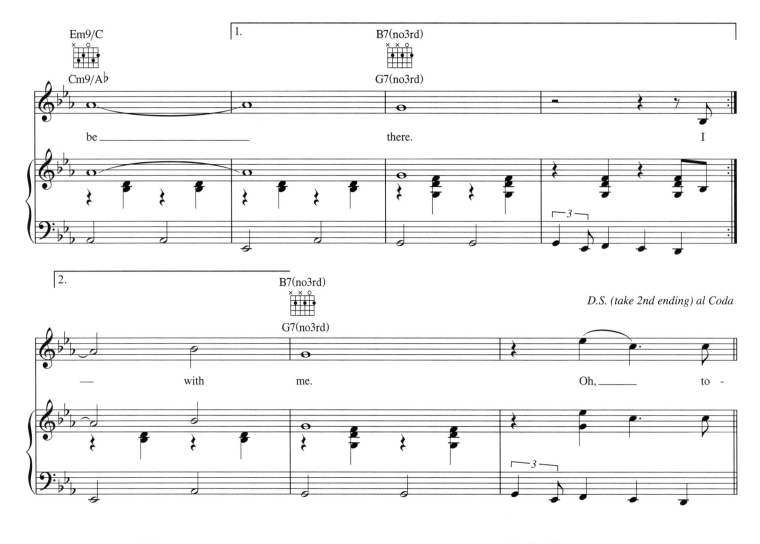

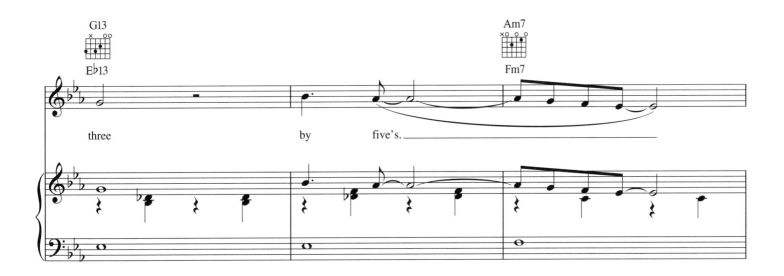

three by five's. _____

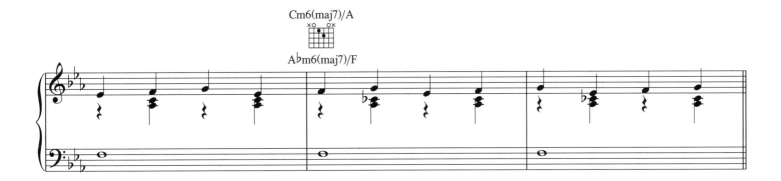

Play 3 times

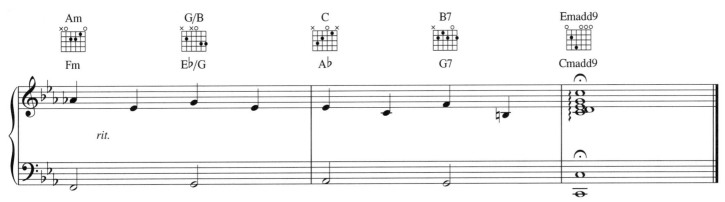

rit.

Love Song for No One

Words by John Mayer

Music by John Mayer
and Clay Cook

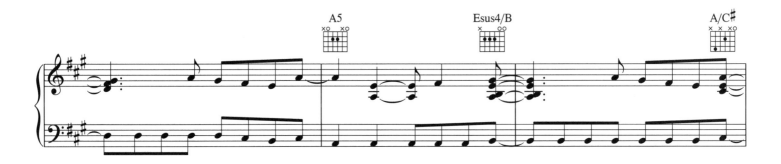

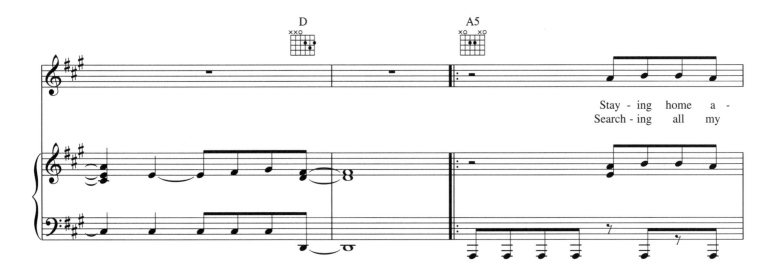

Stay - ing home a -
Search - ing all my

lone on a Fri - day, ___
days just to find you, ___

flat on the floor look - ing back on
I'm not sure who I'm look - ing for.

on
I'll

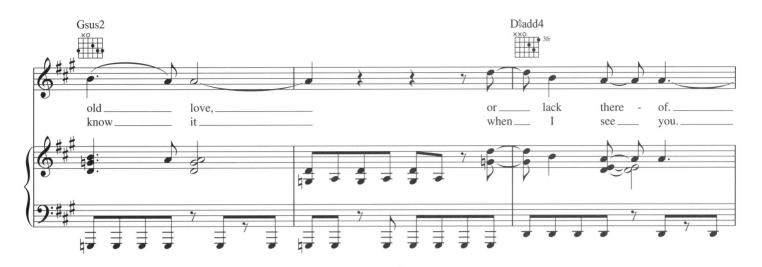

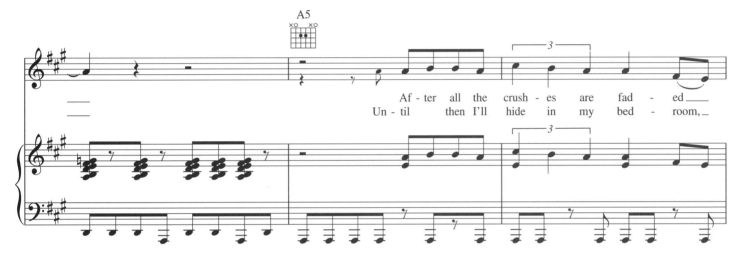

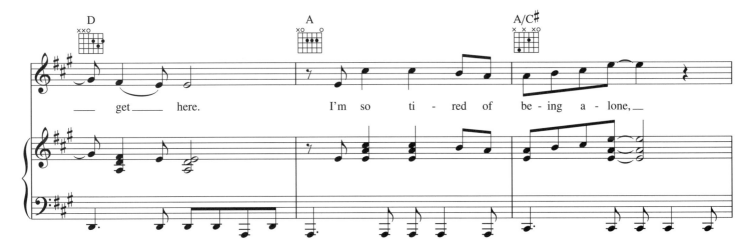

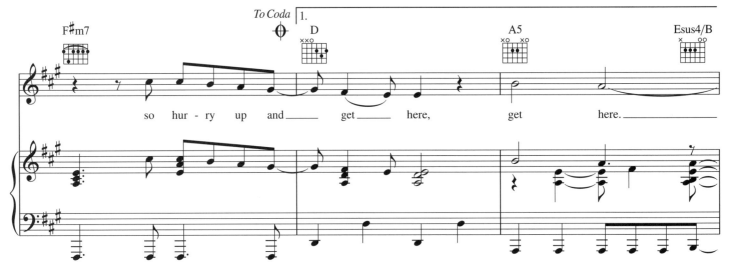

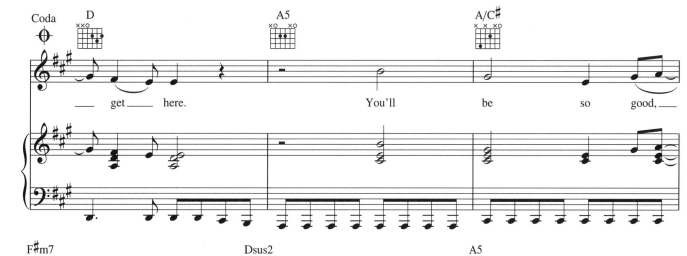

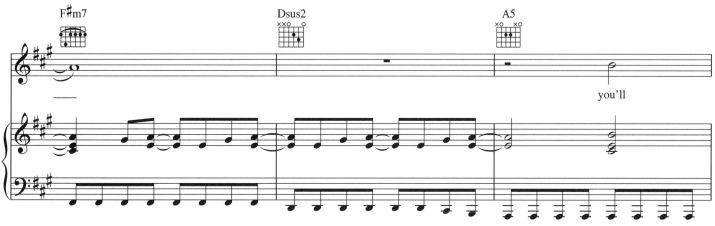

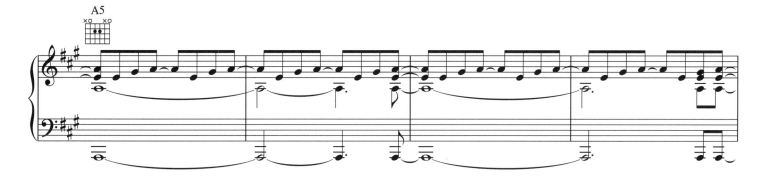

Back to You

Words and Music by
John Mayer

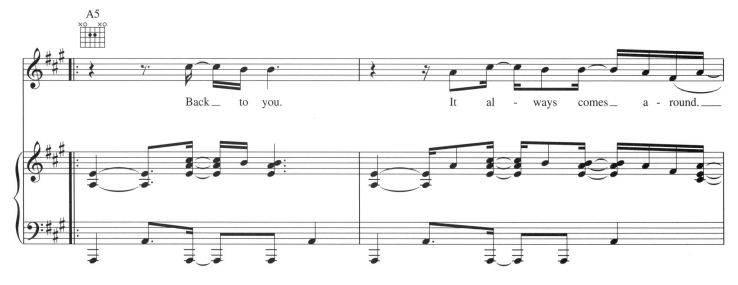

Back___ to you.

It al - ways comes___ a - round.___

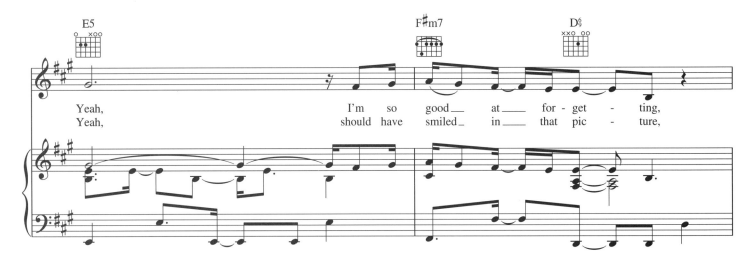

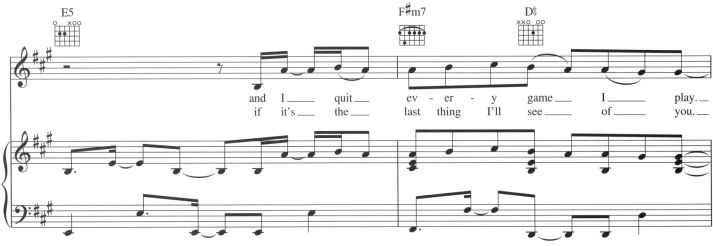

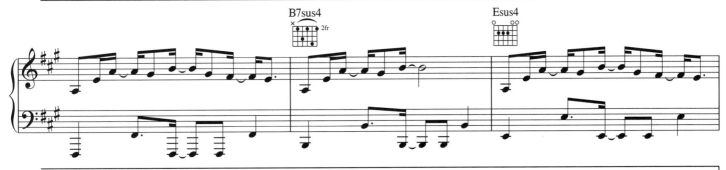

could not do.

Ah.

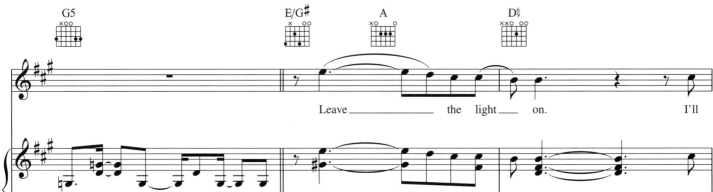

Leave the light on. I'll

nev - er give up on you. Leave the light

Repeat and fade

84

Great Indoors

Words and Music by
John Mayer

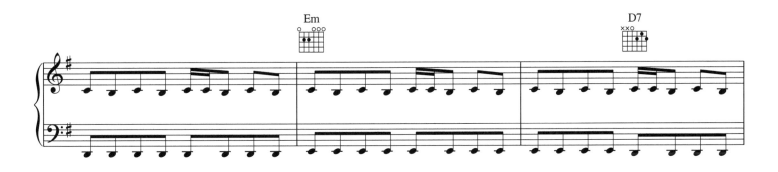

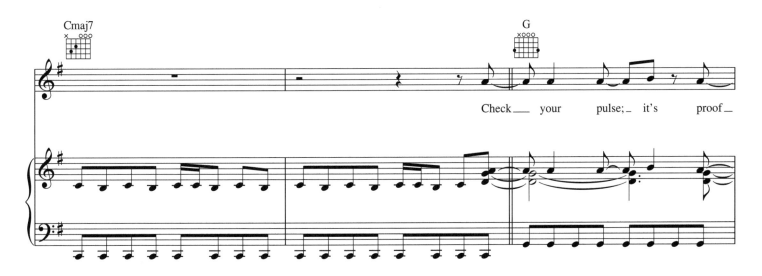

Check___ your pulse;___ it's proof___ ___ that you're___ not lis - ten - ing to the call___ your life's___ been is -

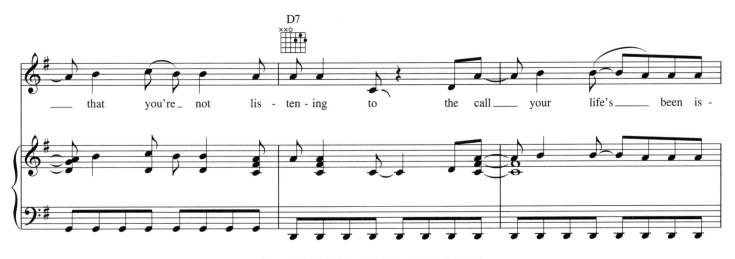

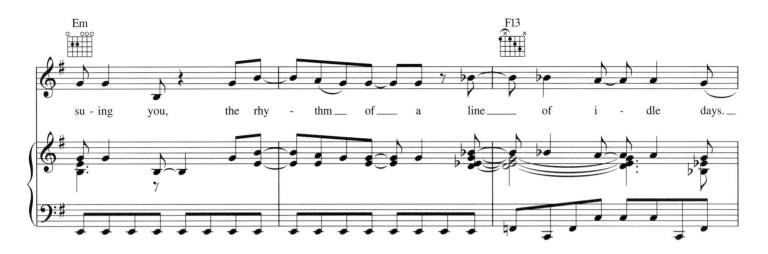

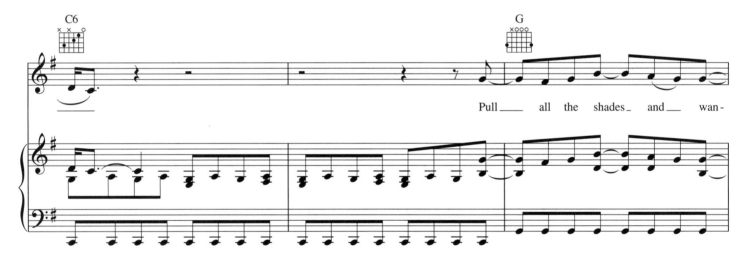

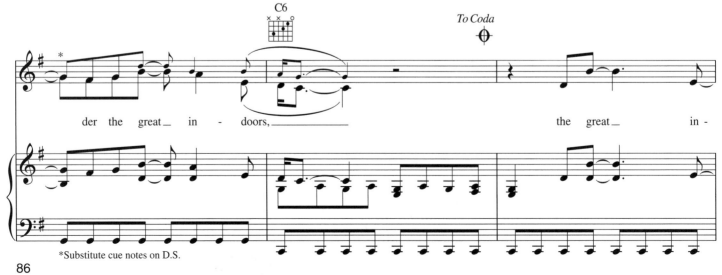

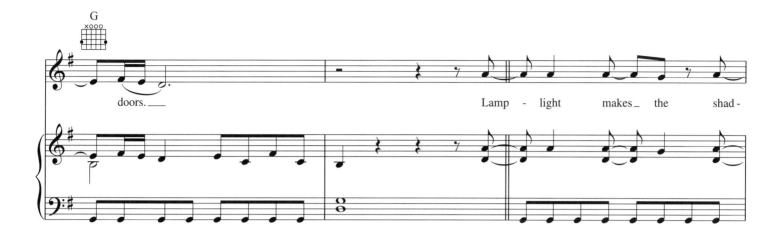

doors. ___ Lamp - light makes ___ the shad-

ows play and post - ers take ___ the walls ___ a - way. ___ The T-

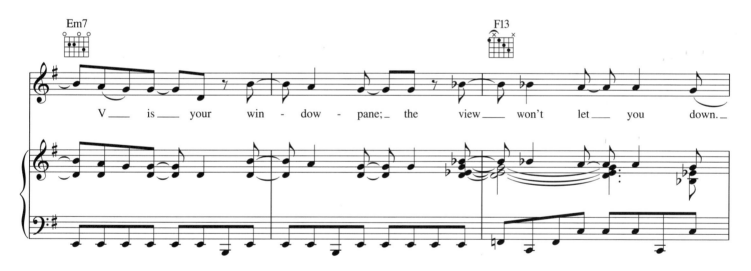

V ___ is ___ your win - dow - pane; the view ___ won't let ___ you down. ___

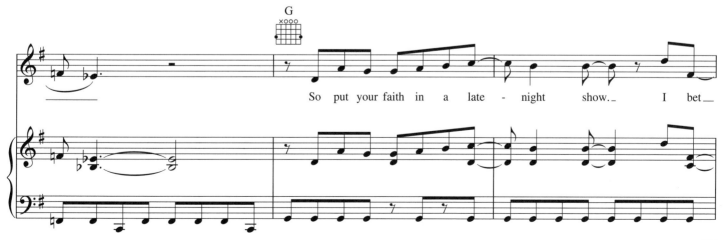

So put your faith in a late - night show. ___ I bet ___

you did-n't e-ven know. De-pends on how far out

Em7

D7

F13

D.S. al Coda

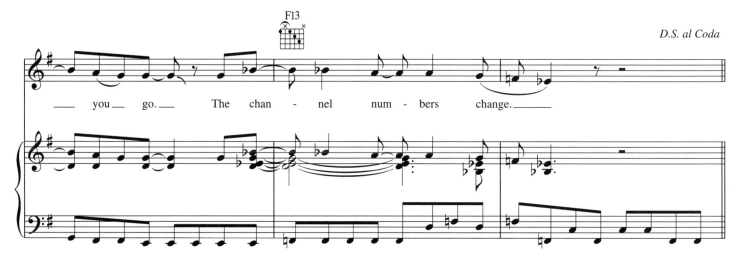

you go. The chan-nel num-bers change.

Coda

Cm6

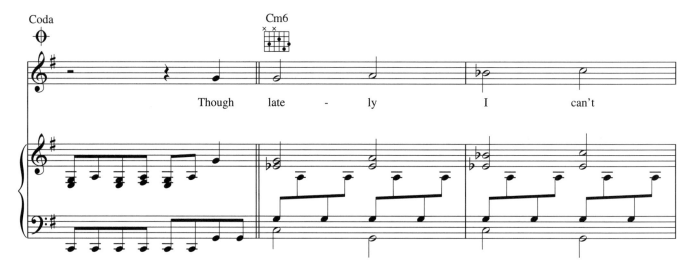

Though late-ly I can't

Emadd9

D

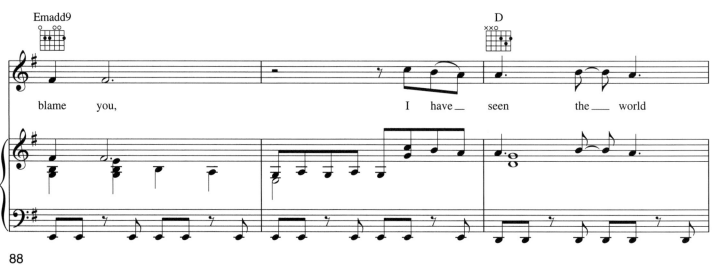

blame you, I have seen the world

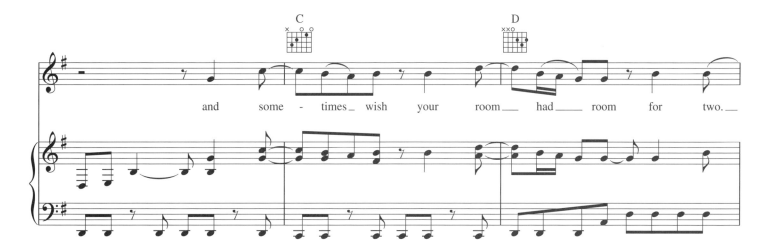

and some - times_ wish your room_ had_ room for two._

_ Da _ da da da _ da.

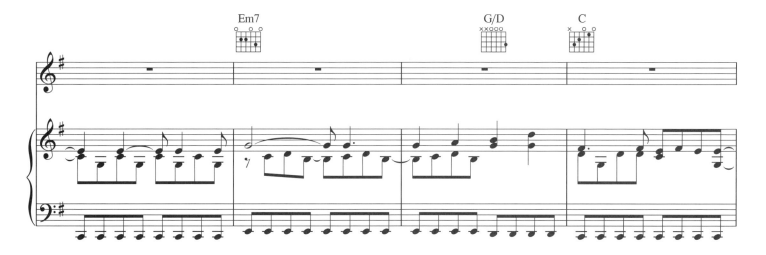

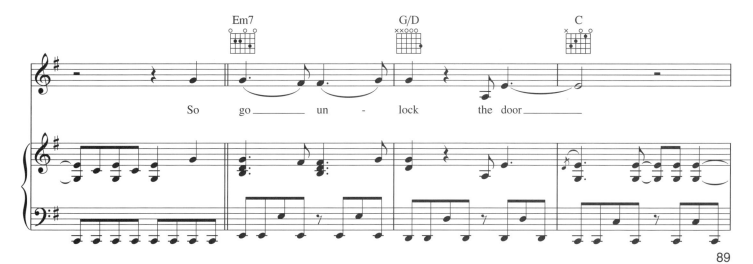

So go _ un - lock the door_

and find _____ what _____ you are here _____ for. Leave _____

_____ the great _____ in - doors, _____ leave the great _____ in - doors. _____

_____ _____ Di oo di _____ ya di _____ ya di _____

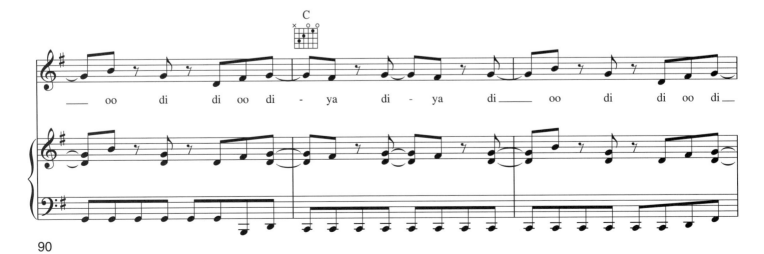

_____ oo di di oo di - ya di - ya di _____ oo di di oo di _____

Not Myself

Words and Music by
John Mayer

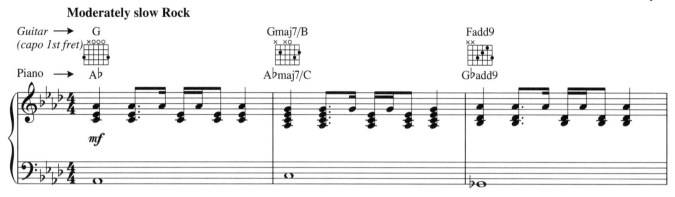

Sup - pose   I ___ said ___   I ___
Sup - pose   I ___ said ___   col -

___ am on my   best ___ be - hav - ior,   and there   are ___ times ___
ors change for   no ___ good rea - son,   and words   will ___ go ___

I lose __ my __ wor - ried mind. __
from po - et - ry __ to prose. Would __

Chorus

__ you want __ me when __ I'm not __ my - self?

Wait __ it out __ while I __ am some - one else? __

And

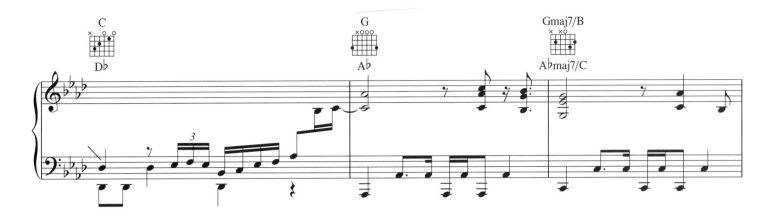

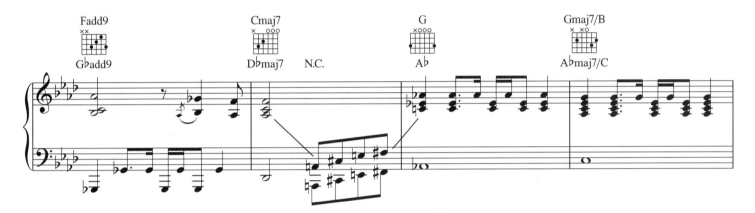

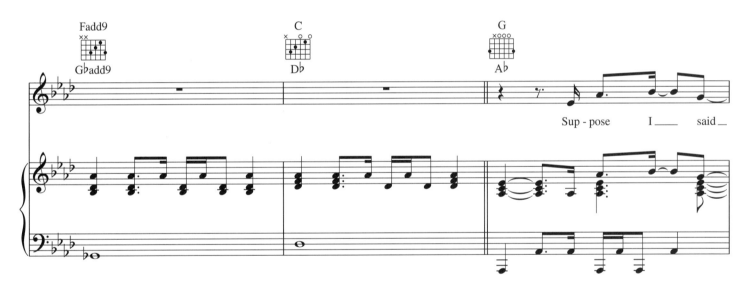

Sup - pose I ___ said ___

D.S. and fade on Chorus

___ you're ___ my sav - ing grace? _____ Would ___

St. Patrick's Day

Words and Music by
John Mayer

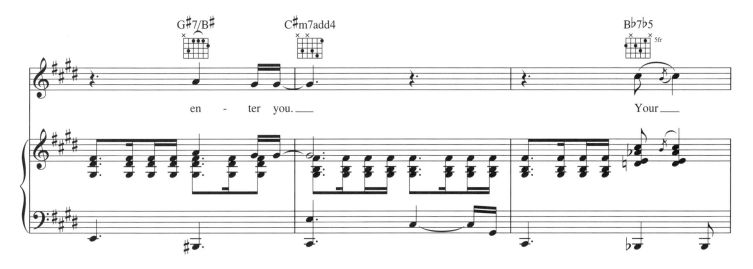

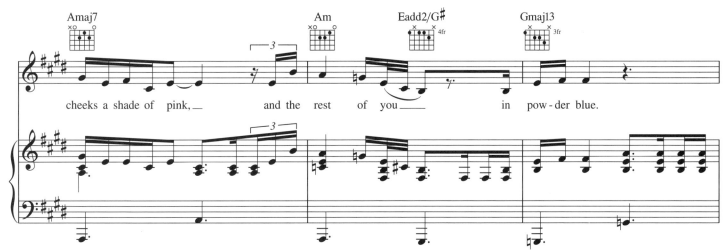

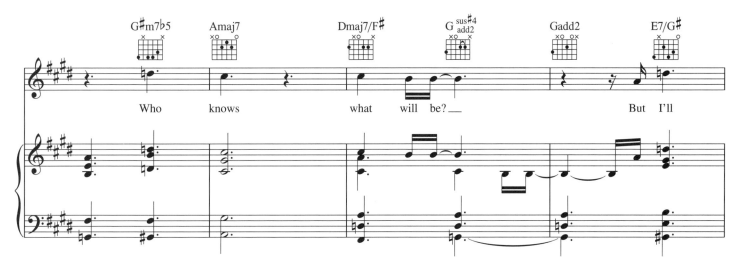

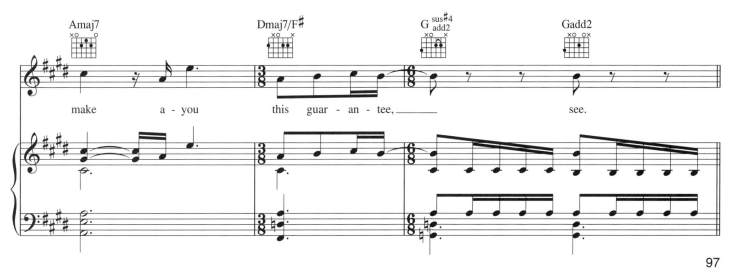

No way No-vem-ber will see our good-bye.___ When it comes___ to De-cem-ber___ it's

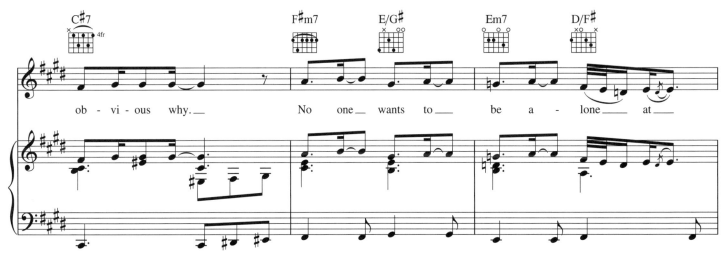

ob-vi-ous why.___ No one___ wants to___ be a-lone___ at___

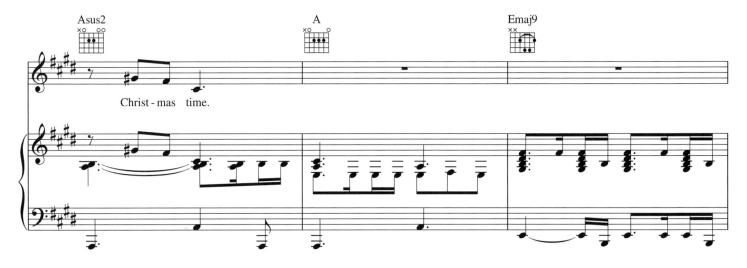

Christ-mas time.

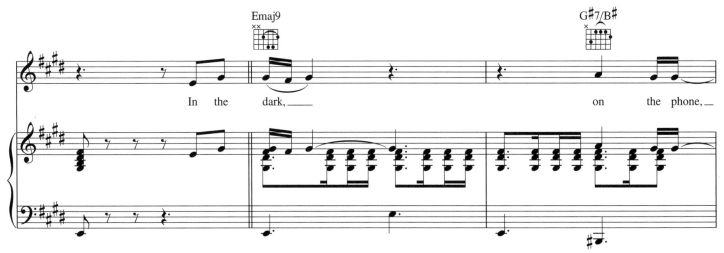

In the dark,____ on the phone,__

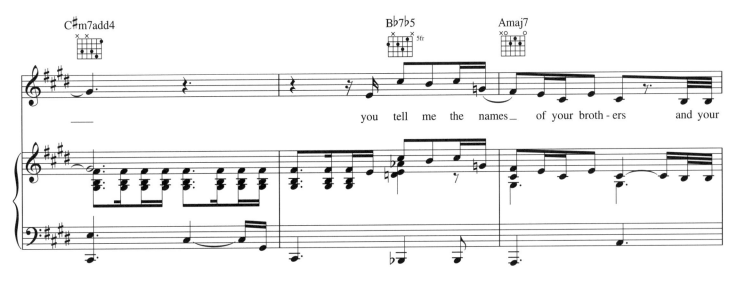

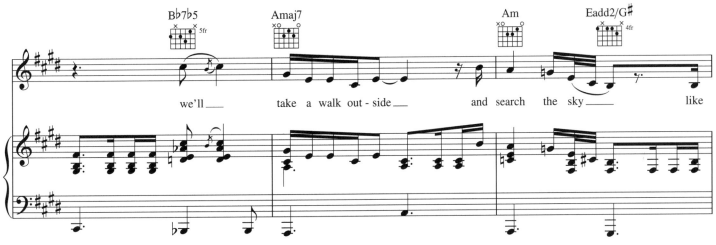

chil - dren do.   I'll say to you: No way No - vem - ber will

me.   *Vocal ad lib...*

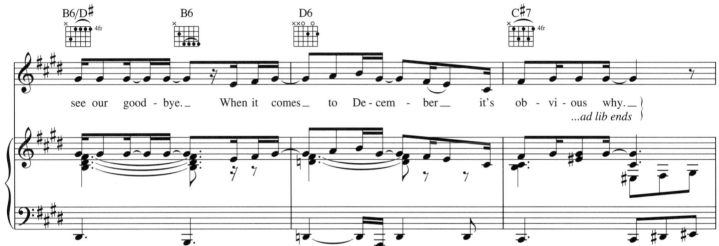

see our good - bye.   When it comes to De - cem - ber   it's ob - vi - ous why.

...ad lib ends

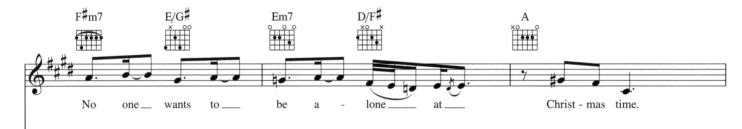

No one wants to be a - lone at   Christ - mas time.

And come Jan - u - ar - y we're fro - zen in - side, mak - ing new

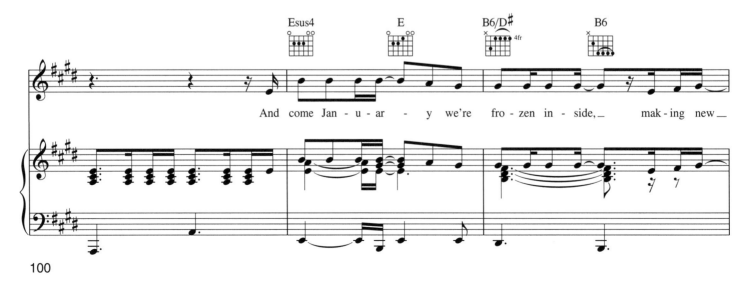

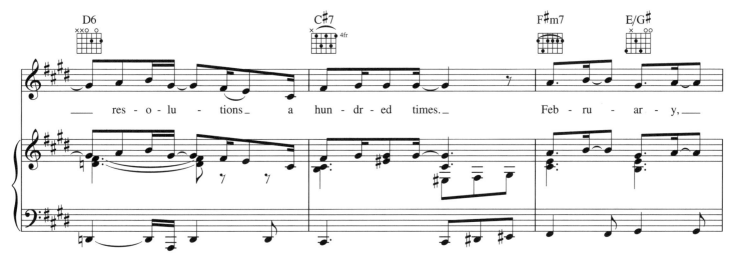

res - o - lu - tions __ a hun - dr - ed times. __ Feb - ru - ar - y, __

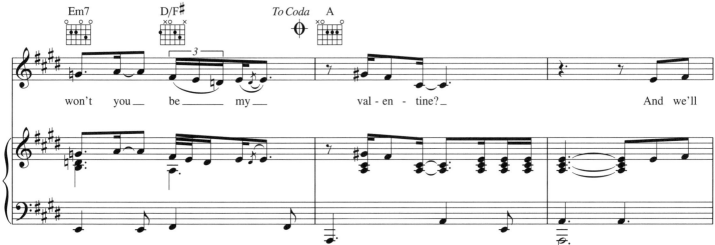

won't you __ be _____ my __ val - en - tine? __ And we'll

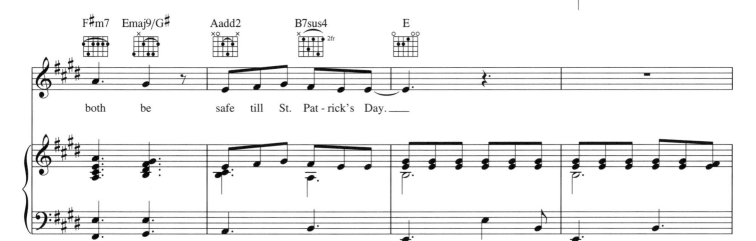

both be safe till St. Pat - rick's Day. ___

We should take a ride to - night a - round the town and

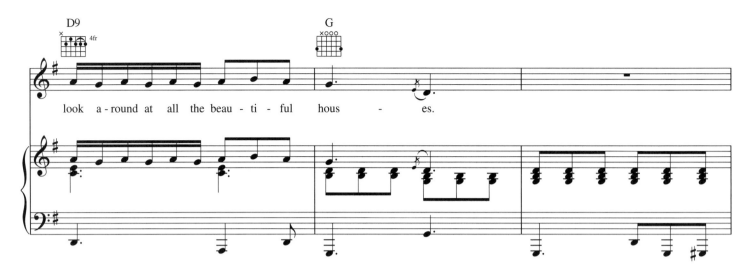

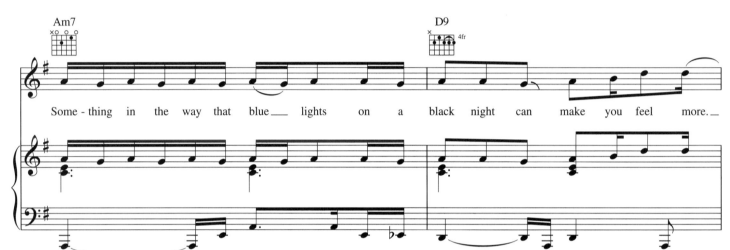

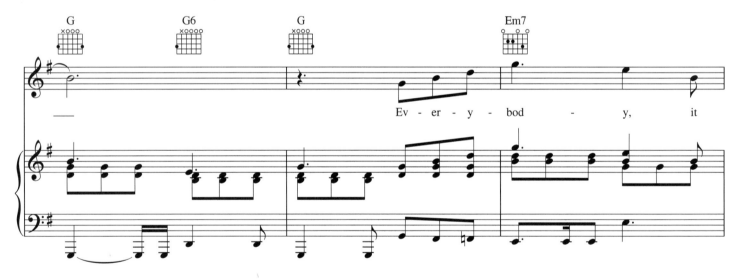

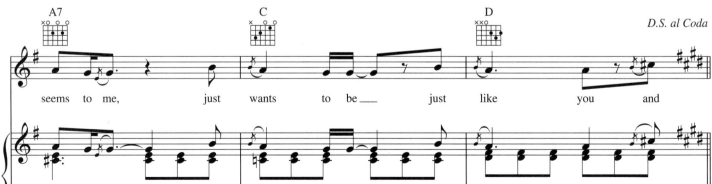

val - en - tine? _ And if our al - ways is

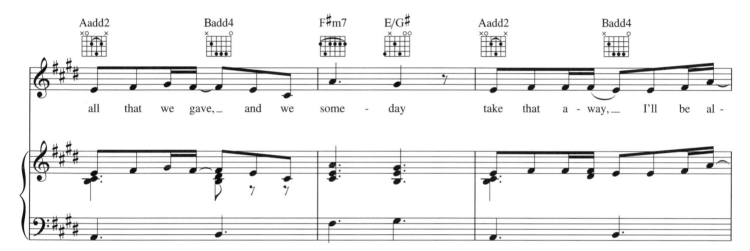

all that we gave, _ and we some - day take that a - way, _ I'll be al -

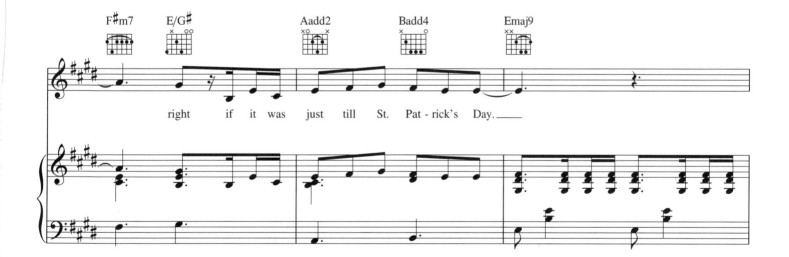

right if it was just till St. Pat - rick's Day. ____

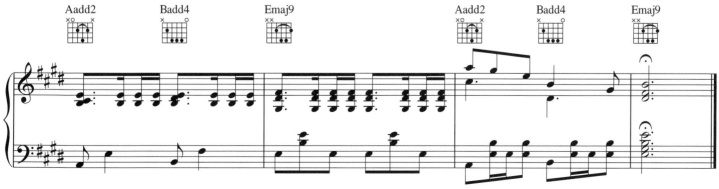

More Great Piano/Vocal Books from Cherry Lane

For a complete listing of Cherry Lane titles available, including contents listings, please visit our web site at
www.cherrylane.com

02500343	Almost Famous	$14.95
02501801	Amistad	$14.95
02502171	The Best of Boston	$17.95
02500144	Mary Chapin Carpenter – Party Doll and Other Favorites	$16.95
02502163	Mary Chapin Carpenter – Stones in the Road	$17.95
02502165	John Denver Anthology – Revised	$22.95
02502227	John Denver – A Celebration of Life	$14.95
02500002	John Denver Christmas	$14.95
02502166	John Denver's Greatest Hits	$17.95
02502151	John Denver – A Legacy in Song (Softcover)	$24.95
02502152	John Denver – A Legacy in Song (Hardcover)	$34.95
02500326	John Denver – The Wildlife Concert	$17.95
02509922	The Songs of Bob Dylan	$29.95
02500396	Linda Eder – Christmas Stays the Same	$17.95
02500175	Linda Eder – It's No Secret Anymore	$14.95
02502209	Linda Eder – It's Time	$17.95
02509912	Erroll Garner Songbook, Vol. 1	$17.95
02500270	Gilbert & Sullivan for Easy Piano	$12.95
02500318	Gladiator	$12.95
02500273	Gold & Glory: The Road to El Dorado	$16.95
02502126	Best of Guns N' Roses	$17.95
02502072	Guns N' Roses – Selections from Use Your Illusion I and II	$17.95
02500014	Sir Roland Hanna Collection	$19.95
02502134	Best of Lenny Kravitz	$12.95
02500012	Lenny Kravitz – 5	$16.95
02500381	Lenny Kravitz – Greatest Hits	$14.95
02500003	Dave Matthews Band – Before These Crowded Streets	$17.95
02502199	Dave Matthews Band – Crash	$17.95
02502192	Dave Matthews Band – Under the Table and Dreaming	$17.95
02500081	Natalie Merchant – Ophelia	$14.95
02500423	Natalie Merchant – Tigerlily	$14.95
02502204	The Best of Metallica	$17.95
02500407	O-Town	$14.95
02500010	Tom Paxton – The Honor of Your Company	$17.95
02507962	Peter, Paul & Mary – Holiday Concert	$17.95
02500145	Pokemon 2.B.A. Master	$12.95
02500026	The Prince of Egypt	$16.95
02502189	The Bonnie Raitt Collection	$22.95

02502230	Bonnie Raitt – Fundamental	$17.95
02502139	Bonnie Raitt – Longing in Their Hearts	$16.95
02502088	Bonnie Raitt – Luck of the Draw	$14.95
02507958	Bonnie Raitt – Nick of Time	$14.95
02502190	Bonnie Raitt – Road Tested	$24.95
02502218	Kenny Rogers – The Gift	$16.95
02500072	Saving Private Ryan	$14.95
02500197	SHeDAISY – The Whole SHeBANG	$14.95
02500414	SHREK	$14.95
02500166	Steely Dan – Anthology	$17.95
02500284	Steely Dan – Two Against Nature	$14.95
02500165	Best of Steely Dan	$14.95
02502132	Barbra Streisand – Back to Broadway	$19.95
02507969	Barbra Streisand – A Collection: Greatest Hits and More	$17.95
02502164	Barbra Streisand – The Concert	$22.95
02502228	Barbra Streisand – Higher Ground	$16.95
02500196	Barbra Streisand – A Love Like Ours	$16.95
02500280	Barbra Streisand – Timeless	$22.95
02503617	John Tesh – Avalon	$15.95
02502178	The John Tesh Collection	$17.95
02503623	John Tesh – A Family Christmas	$15.95
02505511	John Tesh – Favorites for Easy Piano	$12.95
02503630	John Tesh – Grand Passion	$16.95
02500124	John Tesh – One World	$14.95
02500307	John Tesh – Pure Movies 2	$16.95
02502175	Tower of Power – Silver Anniversary	$17.95
02502198	The "Weird Al" Yankovic Anthology	$17.95
02502217	Trisha Yearwood – A Collection of Hits	$16.95
02500334	Maury Yeston – December Songs	$17.95
02502225	The Maury Yeston Songbook	$19.95

See your local music dealer or contact:

CHERRY LANE MUSIC COMPANY
6 East 32nd Street, New York, NY 10016

EXCLUSIVELY DISTRIBUTED BY
HAL•LEONARD® CORPORATION
7777 W. BLUEMOUND RD. P.O. BOX 13819 MILWAUKEE, WI 53213

Prices, contents and availability subject to change without notice.

0402